It doesn't matter
abt. what I see,
that I have faith
& He never A's & answers
I have Victory in Him & will
be with Him!

whatever causes tranquility causes
creativity!

WALKING IN THE
FRUIT OF THE
Spirit

Faith
&
Patience the
Inherit the
Promises! Heb 6:12

I hang in & hang-on!

Bondage, all our-behaviors
are learned
B4 Christ, are learned
behaviors.
IN CHrIST we have a
new nature &
imitate Father too!

WALKING IN THE FRUIT OF THE

Spirit

RELEASING THE NATURE AND POWER OF GOD IN YOUR LIFE

GLORIA COPELAND

Unless otherwise noted, all scripture is from the *King James Version* of the Bible.

Scripture quotations marked AMPC are from the *Amplified Bible, Classic Edition, Amplified Bible* © 1954, 1958, 1962, 1964, 1965, 1987 by The Lockman Foundation. Used by permission.

Scripture quotations marked AMP are from the *Amplified Bible* © 2015 by The Lockman Foundation. Used by permission.

Scripture quotations marked TLB are from *The Living Bible* © 1971. Used by permission of Tyndale House Publishers Inc., Wheaton, IL 60189. All rights reserved.

Scripture quotations marked NIV are from *The Holy Bible, New International Version* © 1973, 1978, 1984, 2011 by Biblica Inc. Used by permission. All rights reserved worldwide.

Scripture quotations marked NKJV are from the *New King James Version* © 1982 by Thomas Nelson Inc.

Scripture quotations marked NLT are from the *Holy Bible, New Living Translation* © 1996, 2004, 2007 by Tyndale Charitable Trust. Used by permission of Tyndale House Publishers.

Scripture quotations marked NASB are from the *New American Standard Bible* © 1960, 1962, 1963, 1968, 1971, 1972, 1973, 1975, 1977, 1995 by the Lockman Foundation. Used by permission.

Walking in the Fruit of the Spirit
Releasing the Nature and Power of God in Your Life

© 2021 Gloria Copeland

ISBN 13 TP: 978-1-60463-422-8 KCM ID: 30-0584
ISBN 13 ePub: 978-1-60463-425-9 KCM ID: 31-0584
ISBN 13 LP: 978-1-60463-424-2 KCM ID: 30-0585
ISBN 13 .mobi: 978-1-60463-426-6 KCM ID: 31-1584

Published by Harrison House Publishers
Shippensburg, PA 17257

Kenneth Copeland Publications
Fort Worth, TX 76192-0001

For more information about Kenneth Copeland Ministries, visit kcm.org or call

1-800-600-7395 (U.S. only) or +1-817-852-6000.

5 6 7 8 / 25 24 23 22 21

CONTENTS

Chapter 1

SUPERNATURAL FORCES OF DIVINE LIFE

But the fruit of the Spirit is love, joy, peace,
longsuffering, gentleness, goodness, faith, meekness,
temperance: against such there is no law.

GALATIANS 5:22-23

The fruit of the spirit are powerful spiritual forces. They're more than just nice character traits for Christians to have. They are our daily victory. Walking in the fruit of the spirit actually opens the door for us, as believers, to walk in the gifts of the Spirit. Love, joy, peace, goodness and kindness are all supernatural expressions of the character and presence of God who lives inside us. When we yield to them, the Holy Spirit enhances and strengthens them in us to become a river of living water that flows out of us to help bless others!

Each fruit of the re-created human spirit supplies us with something we need so we can walk in the blessings and wholeness that Jesus provided for us. And each one provides us with an element of divine power that equips us to meet the challenges of life and come through in victory.

These fruit are born into us when we receive Jesus as our Savior and Lord in the new birth (1 Peter 1:23). They give us the power we need to rise above the snares of the devil and the pull of this fallen world. They help us fulfill our divine calling and keep us strong and stable enough to complete our God-appointed race on this earth. When we're ready to go to heaven, like the Apostle Paul, we can say, "I have fought a good fight, I have finished my course, I have kept the faith: Henceforth there is laid up for me a crown of righteousness, which the Lord, the righteous judge, shall give me at that day: and not to me only, but unto all them also that love his appearing" (2 Timothy 4:7-8).

Without walking in the fruit of the spirit, the gifts of the Spirit won't work. Galatians 5:6 says that faith works by love. So without the spiritual fruit of love, your faith won't work. And "without faith," as Hebrews 11:6 says, "it is impossible to please him."

Nothing the devil comes up with can defeat you when you're walking in the fullness of the fruit! As author Greg Zoschak puts it, "There is not any situation, trial or temptation that a child of God will face that one of the fruit of the spirit will not enable him to overcome."[1]

If the devil tries to stir up trouble in your relationships, for instance, forces like love and kindness will come to your aid. If he tries to discourage you with contrary circumstances, forces like faith and patience will see you through. If he tempts you to get into pride because you're excelling on the job, or to get into fear and turmoil because you're in danger of being laid off, the fruit of humility and peace will protect you.

---

1   Greg Zoschak, *A Call for Character: Developing the Fruit of the Spirit in Your Life* (Tulsa: Harrison House Publishers, 1991) p. 22.

On the other hand, if one of the fruit is not operating in your life, you can't be totally successful because that particular area will be the place where the enemy will concentrate his attack. Without the force of self-control, for example, even though you may have all the other spiritual fruit in operation, without that fruit to help you rein in your natural desires, you'll be vulnerable to getting pulled off course by the lusts of your flesh.

That's why, throughout the New Testament, God tells us continually to cultivate *all* the fruit of the spirit! He loves us and wants us to be overcomers. And that's what the fruit empower us to do.

I first began learning about the fruit of the spirit in 1988, a few weeks before our annual West Coast Believers' Convention. I'd been fellowshipping with the Lord in preparation for the meetings and, as always, I asked Him, "Lord, what do You want me to preach?"

It usually takes a few days for me to discern what He's saying. I have to listen to my spirit for a while until I'm sure I've heard clearly from Him. But that morning was different. He spoke to me so powerfully, I heard Him right away:

I want you to teach on the fruit of the spirit, He said.

His answer totally surprised me. I'd never taught just on the fruit of the spirit. So I began an organized, in-depth study on it. I knew I'd received the Lord's direction, so I dove in and got started!

I began searching my Bible, looking at the many scriptures that talk about the fruit of the spirit, and I got some wonderful books on the subject. Then, with all my resources piled around me, I read and prayed—hour after hour, day after day—and let the Holy Spirit teach me what you're about to read.

What the Lord showed me not only blessed me, it changed my perception in a way that has impacted my life ever since.

The fruit of the spirit will produce a strong foundation for victory.

I don't know about you, but I want to finish my life as a winner. When reward day comes, I want to hear Jesus say, "Well done, My good and faithful servant!"

I'm sure you do, too. For that to happen, though, we'll need to keep growing consistently in the fruit of the spirit.

Partakers of the Divine Nature

"How exactly do we go about walking consistently in the power of the fruit of the spirit?" you might ask.

The first thing we do is go to the Bible to see what God has to say about the subject. One passage I've studied quite a bit is 2 Peter 1:3-11. It says that God:

> [By] His divine power hath given unto us all things that pertain unto life and godliness, through the knowledge of him that hath called us to glory and virtue: whereby are given unto us exceeding great and precious promises: that by these [we] might be partakers of the divine nature, having escaped the corruption that is in the world through lust (verses 3-4).

These verses help us understand the process by telling us that *godliness* (which is another way to describe the fruit) comes through the knowledge of the Lord.

God has already provided every born-again believer with everything it takes to bear spiritual fruit.

The better we get to *know Him,* the greater revelation we'll have of His divine nature that's already inside us. The better we understand His nature, the more we can partake of it, and the freer of this world's corruption we become.

The passage goes on to say:

> And beside this, giving all diligence, add to your faith virtue; and to virtue knowledge; and to knowledge temperance; and to temperance patience; and to patience godliness; and to godliness brotherly kindness; and to brotherly kindness charity. For if these things be in you, and abound, they make you that ye shall neither be barren nor unfruitful in the knowledge of our Lord Jesus Christ.... Wherefore the rather, brethren, give diligence to make your calling and election sure: for if ye do these things, ye shall never fall: For so an entrance shall be ministered unto you abundantly into the everlasting kingdom of our Lord and Saviour Jesus Christ (verses 5-8, 10-11).

If you ever need inspiration to walk in the fruit of the spirit, reread those verses often. They list many wonderful benefits. When you abound in the fruit, you enter into the best God has planned for you. Operating in them empowers you to fulfill your divine call. You'll remain spiritually surefooted and avoid destructive falls. Best of all, according to these verses, when you've finished your earthly assignment, you'll enjoy an abundant entrance into God's everlasting kingdom!

What does it mean to have an abundant entrance into His kingdom?

For one thing, it means you won't just barely make it into heaven by the skin of your teeth. And, you won't get there empty-handed with nothing to show for the life you lived here. When you step out of this natural realm into the glory realm, because you cultivated and walked in the fruit of the spirit here on earth, you'll have eternal rewards awaiting you. You'll have a big welcoming party gathered there to greet you.

Lots of people will be flocking around you telling you how glad they are to see you. You'll have family members and friends there. People you've loved and ministered to will be celebrating your arrival in heaven and telling you how, while they were on earth, they were influenced by all the fruit of the spirit they saw in your life!

The Fruit + the Gifts = Maximum Power

The gifts of the Spirit are exciting and spectacular, and the Church definitely needs them (1 Corinthians 12:7-11). They're extremely valuable. But unlike the fruit, the gifts don't manifest whenever you want them to. You can't get up every morning and say, "I believe I'll walk in the word of wisdom and the gift of miracles today."

No, the gifts manifest only as the Holy Spirit wills (1 Corinthians 12:11). They function only in certain situations. You can't live on the gifts. People who try end up getting into trouble.

We've all heard the stories. We've heard about tongue-talking Christians who regularly prophesied in church on Sundays and yet, somehow, ended up falling into a lifestyle of sin. We've even heard, on occasion, about a truly anointed minister of God who had great healings and miracles taking place in his or her meetings and then got involved in some kind of illicit affair. What opened the door to those tragedies? How could such seemingly spiritual believers end up going so wrong?

The answer is simple. *Those believers operated in spiritual gifts, but they didn't have much spiritual fruit.* So they didn't have the strength to overcome the pressures of temptation. As a result, when the devil came after them, they succumbed to his attack. They ended up going on a fleshly detour that left them shipwrecked and robbed them of part of God's purpose for their lives.

No believer ever intends to end up that way! But if we don't learn to walk in the power of our divine nature, it can happen to any of us. That's why we don't want to put all our focus on the gifts. Although it's scriptural and good to "covet earnestly" the gifts (1 Corinthians 12:31), we also should want to *covet and cultivate the fruit.*

- We want the love of God flowing in abundance because "love never fails" (1 Corinthians 13:8, NKJV).
- We want plenty of joy because "the joy of the Lord is your strength" (Nehemiah 8:10).
- We want peace because it keeps us tranquil in times of trouble.
- We want faith and patience because they're the power twins that undergird us so when we're believing God for healing or prosperity or something else He's promised, we're able to hang in there until we receive.
- We want gentleness, goodness and meekness because they enhance our relationships, and empower us to manifest to those around us the character and life of God.
- We want temperance, or self-control, because it comes to our aid and gives us victory in our conflicts with the world, the flesh and the devil.

The maximum manifestation of spiritual power is achieved in our lives only when the gifts and the fruit are working together. So value *both* the gifts and the fruit. Desire to move in the gifts as the Holy Spirit wills, and develop your faith to walk consistently in all the fruit as well. You'll be setting yourself up to be a winner in every aspect of life!

Witnesses of the Power and Character of Christ

You won't be the only one who wins as a result of the fruit of the spirit you bear. Others will benefit, too. As the forces of God's divine nature flow through you, you'll become a greater blessing and bring change into the lives of people around you. You'll impact the world in a greater way for Jesus and, as believers, that's what we're called to do.

We're called to be witnesses to the power of our resurrected Savior with our words but also to reveal Him through who we are and what we do. Acts 1:8 says, "But ye shall receive power, after that the Holy Ghost is come upon you: and ye shall be witnesses unto me both in Jerusalem, and in all Judaea, and in Samaria, and unto the uttermost part of the earth."

We're called to be a living revelation of God's love, life and divine character.

At this very moment, people all over this earth are starving for a revelation of God's love and goodness. They're hungry to "taste and see that the Lord is good" (Psalm 34:8). They may not realize it, but they're craving the fruit of the spirit that's available only through a personal relationship with God.

Everyone in the world wants to be loved. Even seemingly hardened sinners who haven't heard or believed the gospel are seeking joy and peace. But they're looking in the wrong place. The world can't provide those things.

The world has no real victory to offer. It can't help people when they're in a crisis or provide the solution when their marriages are crumbling, their bodies and emotions are breaking down under the stresses of life, or they're being driven to destruction by fleshly lusts they can't control.

Even the so-called "success strategies" the world comes up with can't produce real or lasting success, because apart from Jesus, it's not available. Without Him, people have no way to truly live as overcomers. They can't access supernatural forces like love, joy, peace, patience, gentleness, goodness, faithfulness, meekness and self-control, so they don't have the power to triumph over the troubles of life.

But we can help them find that power! We can share with them the good news about Jesus and show them the abundant life He provides. We can point them to the Answer Himself by cultivating and yielding to His nature, making it our lifestyle, and putting it on display.

Simply by walking in the fruit of the spirit on purpose, every day, wherever we go, we can let the world see Jesus in us!

Speak Your Faith

I declare by faith that I walk in the fruit of the spirit that are in me because God's divine nature lives in me. It is making me an overcomer in every area of my life. I walk in love, joy, peace, longsuffering (patience), gentleness, goodness, faith, meekness and temperance (self-control). I am a living revelation to others of God's love, life and divine character!

Chapter 2

LIVING LIKE WHO YOU REALLY ARE

...Walk not after the flesh, but after the Spirit. For they that are after the flesh do mind the things of the flesh; but they that are after the Spirit the things of the Spirit.

ROMANS 8:4-5

If you're a born-again believer, all the fruit of the spirit are already within you. As we learned, they were born into you when you put your faith in Jesus. The moment you received Him as your Lord and were born again, you became a partaker of His divine nature. Really, that's what the fruit of the spirit are—the manifestation of the nature of God that's inside you.

The fruit of the spirit are not just something you *do*. They are the expression of your true identity as a child of God. They are who you *are* because it's who He is.

Love is a fruit of the spirit because "God is Love" (1 John 4:8).

Goodness, kindness and patience are fruit of the spirit because "he is good [and] his mercy endureth forever" (Psalm 118:1).

Joy is a fruit of the spirit because God is joyful. He laughs and rejoices with gladness (Psalm 2:4, NLT; Zephaniah 3:17).

The fruit of the spirit abound in God! They are His nature. And since we've been re-created in His image, we can be confident we have an abundance of them, too. We can rest assured that because the Spirit of Christ is in us, all the forces of His divine life are in us, as well. They've been implanted into our spirits through our union with Him.

The fruit of the spirit are the supernatural, natural outflow of a born-again, Holy Spirit-controlled life.

"Why do I need to study about the fruit, then? Don't they just flow out of my spirit without me even having to think about it?"

It's because your spirit isn't the only thing you have to deal with. You also have to deal with your flesh. Your flesh has to be taught and trained to yield and cooperate with the forces in your re-created spirit so that it conforms to your new spiritual identity.

Although your spirit was transformed instantly into God's image when you were born again, your flesh wasn't. It was the same the moment after you got saved as it was the moment before. It still had all the same old sin-tainted habits.

Those old habits don't reflect your new identity because when you established them, you were an unbeliever. You were still under the influence of the devil and the world. You didn't have the life of God or the fruit of the spirit inside you because you were still "dead in trespasses and sins" (Ephesians 2:1).

That's the condition we were all in before we received Jesus. We were spiritually dead. We all had sinned and "come short of the glory of God" (Romans 3:23) because of the sin of our natural forefather, Adam.

If you've read the book of Genesis, you know Adam disobeyed the one command God gave him in the Garden of Eden. He ate of the tree of the knowledge of good and evil, after God clearly told him, "thou shalt not eat of it: for in the day that thou eatest thereof thou shalt surely die" (Genesis 2:17).

The instant Adam committed that sin, the divine life that was in him departed. He severed his inner connection with God and fell from his place in the realm of the supernatural. He died spiritually and became limited to the natural realm. Although his physical body continued to live for a while, he experienced a dramatically different kind of existence.

Instead of operating in his God-given dominion as ruler over the earth, he became subject to his earthly environment. Instead of walking with God in the light, he had to stumble around in spiritual darkness. He had to lean on his own natural understanding and operate according to what he could physically feel and see. Worst of all, sin ruled in his inner man. The fountain of divine life that had once flowed from within him became a fountain of spiritual death.

Compared to the scope of what God had in mind when He created mankind, Adam's life after he disobeyed God was a pitiful existence!

Even today, it's the only kind of life available apart from Jesus. People who haven't put their faith in Jesus don't have the eternal life of God within them. Although they're alive physically, they haven't been born again of the Holy Spirit, so they aren't partakers of the divine nature.

This is what Jesus was explaining to Nicodemus in John 3:

> Verily, verily, I say unto thee, Except a man be born again, he cannot see the kingdom of God.... That which is born of the flesh is flesh; and that which is born of the Spirit is spirit. Marvel not that I said unto thee, Ye must be born again (verses 3, 6-7).

A New Species of Being

The new birth opens up a whole new life for everyone who receives it! But it also puts those of us who have experienced it in a peculiar situation:

Born-again believers are a unique species of being. We're supernatural spirits living in natural bodies.

We're children of God with His heavenly nature inside us, yet we're still walking around in earth suits made of unspiritual flesh.

When we first start living the Christian life, this presents us with a challenge. On one hand, our flesh still wants to dominate and do the same things it did when we were sinners. On the other hand, our reborn spirits desire to take over and empower us to live God's way. So, with our flesh pulling one direction and our spirits pulling the other, we're caught in a kind of a spiritual tug of war.

So, what do we do to make sure the right side wins?

First, let me tell you what we *don't* do. As New Testament believers, we don't overcome the pull of our flesh by living like people did in the Old Testament. We don't muster up our own natural willpower and try, in our own strength, to conquer our fleshly tendencies to keep God's laws.

That approach *never* succeeds. Trying to deal with our flesh in our own human strength always leads to failure. The flesh can't be brought into line that way. It can only be brought into submission by the nature of God that comes from within us when we allow our spirit man to take dominion.

One group of Christians in the New Testament—the believers in Galatia—learned this the hard way. After they were born again, they made the mistake of striving on their own to live according to Old Testament Law, and the results were disastrous. Their flesh took over, and they got into a mess. To help them get straightened out, the Apostle Paul wrote them a letter: "Walk in the Spirit," he said, "and ye shall not fulfil the lust of the flesh" (Galatians 5:16)! The AMPC says it this way:

> But I say, walk and live [habitually] in the [Holy] Spirit [responsive to and controlled and guided by the Spirit]; then you will certainly not gratify the cravings and desires of the flesh (of human nature without God). For the desires of the flesh are opposed to the [Holy] Spirit, and the [desires of the] Spirit are opposed to the flesh (godless human nature); for these are antagonistic to each other [continually withstanding and in conflict with each other], so that you are not free but are prevented from doing what you desire to do. But if you are guided (led) by the [Holy] Spirit, you are not subject to the [Old Testament] Law. Now the doings (practices) of the flesh are clear (obvious): they are immorality, impurity, indecency, idolatry, sorcery, enmity, strife, jealousy, anger (ill temper), selfishness, divisions (dissensions), party spirit (factions, sects with peculiar opinions, heresies), envy, drunkenness, carousing, and the like. I warn you beforehand, just as I did previously, that those who do such things shall not inherit the kingdom of God. But the fruit of the [Holy] Spirit [the work which His presence within accomplishes] is love, joy (gladness), peace, patience (an even temper, forbearance), kindness, goodness (benevolence), faithfulness, gentleness (meekness, humility), self-control (self-restraint, continence). Against such things there is no law [that can bring a charge]. And those who belong to Christ Jesus (the Messiah) have crucified the flesh (the godless human nature) with its passions and appetites and desires. If we live by the [Holy] Spirit, let us also walk by the Spirit. [If by the Holy Spirit we have our life in

God, let us go forward walking in line, our conduct controlled by the Spirit] (verses 16-25).

When Paul said in that passage, "But if you are guided (led) by the [Holy] Spirit, you are not subject to the [Old Testament] Law," he wasn't saying we should just do whatever we feel like doing and forget about obeying God's commands. No, he was telling us that under the new covenant, we obey God's commandments in a *different* way.

Instead of focusing on the bad things you know you're not supposed to do, focus on fellowshipping with God and walking according to your new inward nature. Practice yielding to your new supernatural personality and following after the part of you that's like your heavenly Father. In the process, you'll wind up keeping His commandments automatically. Your flesh will come into submission to your spirit, and as you "imitate God in everything you do, because you are his dear children" (Ephesians 5:1, NLT), you'll just naturally do His will.

"But Gloria, you don't understand my situation!" someone might say. "I have some really stubborn bad habits. Even though I'm a born-again believer, I don't seem to be able to conquer them."

Yes, you can! You just haven't been tapping into what belongs to you as a child of God. You haven't been releasing your faith in your reborn spiritual identity and investing yourself in your relationship with the Lord. You've been focused on the weakness of your flesh trying, in the natural, to break those bad habits and overcome them yourself.

That way of living is a recipe for frustration! It not only traps you in a cycle of defeat, but it leaves you with a nagging sense of condemnation. It makes you want to say as Paul did in Romans 7:

> ...In me (that is, in my flesh) nothing good dwells; for to will is present with me, but how to perform that which is good I do not find. For the good that I will to do, I do not do; but the evil

I will not to do, that I practice. Now if I do what I will not to do, it is no longer I who do it, but sin that dwells in me. I find then a law, that evil is present with me, the one who wills to do good. For I delight in the law of God according to the inward man. But I see another law in my members, warring against the law of my mind, and bringing me into captivity to the law of sin which is in my members. O wretched man that I am! Who will deliver me from this body of death? (verses 18-24, NKJV).

We can all identify with that passage! Every one of us, at one time or another, has wondered, *How am I ever going to be able to get this stubborn, sin-prone flesh under control?*

What's the answer to that question? Paul gives it to us in the next few verses:

I thank God through Jesus Christ our Lord.... There is therefore now no condemnation to them which are in Christ Jesus, who walk not after the flesh, but after the Spirit. For the law of the Spirit of life in Christ Jesus hath made [us] free from the law of sin and death. For what the law could not do, in that it was weak through the flesh, God sending his own Son in the likeness of sinful flesh, and for sin, condemned sin in the flesh: that the righteousness of the law might be fulfilled in us, who walk not after the flesh, but after the Spirit (Romans 7:25, 8:1-4).

This is the reason you can be confident you have what it takes to walk in victory over your flesh. You're *in* Christ Jesus, and He's in you. He has already won the victory for you!

Jesus went to the cross for you, paid the price for sin, and broke its power over you forever!

Jesus delivered you from the bondage of your sinful flesh and set you free. You might have some sinful habits still trying to cling to your outward man or some old, fleshly tendencies trying to put pressure on you. But you don't have to yield to those things! Sin is no longer operating in your spirit. It was eradicated from your inner man the moment you were born again.

You're no longer under the law of sin and death (Romans 8:2). You have *the law of the spirit of life in Christ Jesus* operating in you that's producing the supernatural forces of the spirit.

As you focus on and allow those forces to flow, they liberate you from the domination of your flesh. They will even rid you of ungodly ways and patterns of thinking.

"But what if I've had those habits and patterns a long time?" you might ask.

It doesn't matter! They aren't part of your new, true identity. They're part of the old man—what you used to be. That old, unregenerate man died when you were born again, and he's never coming back, unless you invite him back.

So let the forces of the spirit flow from within you! Live out of your heart—out of your spirit—as a new creation in Christ Jesus. You're free to "put off concerning the former conversation [manner of living] the old man, which is corrupt according to the deceitful lusts; and be renewed in the spirit of your mind; and...put on the new man, which after God is created in righteousness and true holiness" (Ephesians 4:22-24). You don't have to stay trapped in the old fleshly cycle of defeat anymore!

- You're now a "new creature: old things are passed away; behold, all things are become new" (2 Corinthians 5:17).
- You've been made "the righteousness of God" in Christ Jesus (verse 21).

- You've been raised up and made to "sit together in heavenly places in Christ Jesus" (Ephesians 2:6).

What's more, you have the Holy Spirit living inside you to help you. He has come to forever abide, or live, inside you to be your Strengthener, Teacher and Standby. He's always there to give you an extra boost and to help empower you to live out the life of God that's now within you.

In Christ, you're fully equipped to live in total victory!

Speak Your Faith

I declare that I am a new creature in Christ Jesus. Old things are passed away. The old sin nature has no more dominion over me. All things are become new in me because Jesus is my Lord. I have been made the righteousness of God in Christ (2 Corinthians 5:21). I have been made to sit together with Him in heavenly places in Christ Jesus!

Your Flesh Can Be Trained

I don't mean to suggest, of course, that living a victorious Christian life will always be easy or, in every situation, the fruit of the spirit will just automatically flow. No, to consistently walk in the spirit, you'll have to "fight the good fight of faith" (1 Timothy 6:12), which requires exerting some inner-man strength.

Why? Because, particularly when you first get started, your flesh will resist this new way of operating because it's used to being in control. It's accustomed to calling the shots and doing things the world's way.

As we've already established, however, you're a new creature in Christ. Your flesh doesn't have power over you anymore. It can fuss and try to demand its way, but it's been "crucified...with [its] affections and lusts"

(Galatians 5:24) through the new birth. The dominating power in your life now is your reborn spirit. When you fill your spirit with the power that's in the Word of God, it can rise up and exercise dominion over your flesh. It can now "put to death the misdeeds of the body" and tell it what to do (Romans 8:13, NIV).

When your flesh starts to push you around and tries to make you do something that's against the Word of God, talk to it.

Speak Your Faith

No, flesh! You're not having control of my life. You're not going to push me into those immoral thoughts and actions. You have been crucified, flesh. You have no hold on me! The Holy Spirit lives in me, and I have dominion over you. I am more than a conqueror over you because I am a new creature in Christ Jesus!

The more you do that, the more your flesh will get in line. It will learn what it is allowed to do and not allowed to do. It won't always be trying to pull you off course. Instead, it will eventually just submit and follow along. As you stay in fellowship with God and keep His Word in your eyes, in your ears, in your heart and in your mouth, your spirit will begin to take the lead. You'll be like the believers Hebrews 5:14 talks about, "who by reason of use [or practice] have their senses exercised to discern both good and evil."

Even though your flesh is not born again, you can train it to act on the Word of God. You can exercise dominion over it and practice living from the inside out until you get to the point where your flesh so adapts to spirit-led living that even your physical senses learn to distinguish between good and evil.

When that happens, your body won't be drawn anymore to the old sinful habits that used to enslave you. Your flesh won't crave things like alcohol, cigarettes, sugar and overeating, and your eyes won't want to look at immoral images. Your ears won't want to hear gossip, and your mouth won't want to speak bitter, resentful, ugly words. Your physical faculties will actually withdraw from such things. And your senses, having been trained by your spirit, will be revolted by the works of the flesh and give preference to the things of God.

Sadly, many Christians never experience that kind of maturity because they don't want to do what it takes to get there. Taking the time to fellowship with the Lord in prayer and the Word is the only way to grow in your ability to walk in the spirit. But, the alternative is to continue living a carnal and powerless worldly life.

Spending all your time tending to natural things and catering to the lusts of the flesh will keep you from enjoying the good life of the spirit with its wonderful fruit of love, joy and peace. It will keep you bogged down in the kind of fleshly works we saw listed in Galatians 5:

> Immorality, impure thoughts, eagerness for lustful pleasure, idolatry, participation in demonic activities, hostility, quarreling, jealousy, outbursts of anger, selfish ambition, divisions, the feeling that everyone is wrong except those in your own little group, envy, drunkenness, wild parties, and other kinds of sin (verses 19-21, NLT-96).

All you have to do is read that list to see that living in the flesh is miserable! It's an unhappy lifestyle for anyone—especially for us as believers. It makes us feel like hypocrites because we know on the inside that's not who we really are. And, it makes us unhappy because now we understand that the works of the flesh have negative consequences. Yielding to those fleshly things robs us of the blessings that are ours as children of God and cause us to live far below our rights and privileges in Christ Jesus.

The works of the flesh by themselves can't keep us out of heaven. If we've truly been born again, we'll still go there to be with Jesus when we die. But if we let our flesh stay in control in the meantime, we'll certainly miss out on so many of the wonderful things God had planned for us here on the earth!

We don't want to do that! We want to enjoy all the wonderful things God has provided for us. We want to be the victors God has created us to be—and, praise the Lord, we can do it! We can put our faith in Jesus, walk in the spirit, and live as overcomers through our union with Him.

As Romans says:

> Now if we be dead with Christ, we believe that we shall also live with him: knowing that Christ being raised from the dead dieth no more; death hath no more dominion over him. For in that he died, he died unto sin once: but in that he liveth, he liveth unto God. Likewise reckon ye also yourselves to be dead indeed to sin, but alive unto God through Christ Jesus our Lord. Let not sin therefore reign in your mortal body, that ye should obey it in the lusts thereof. Neither yield ye your members as instruments of unrighteousness unto sin: but yield yourselves unto God, as those that are alive from the dead, and your members as instruments of righteousness unto God.

> ...walk not after the flesh, but after the Spirit. For they that are after the flesh do mind the things of the flesh; but they that are after the Spirit the things of the Spirit. For to be carnally minded is death; but to be spiritually minded is life and peace (Romans 6:8-13, 8:4-6).

Look again at those last few verses. They present a clear choice: We can either live in the deadness of the flesh or in life and peace.

It's an easy choice to make, isn't it?

If you'll learn to live from the inside out, you can put your flesh in its place and reign as a king in life.

If you want life and peace, you can have it! You can walk in the spirit where "sin shall not have dominion over you" (Romans 6:14) and enjoy days of heaven while you're here on earth!

Chapter 3

SOWING THE SEEDS OF ABUNDANT LIFE

If ye then be risen with Christ, seek those things which are above, where Christ sitteth on the right hand of God. Set your affection on things above, not on things on the earth.

COLOSSIANS 3:1-2

The fruit of the spirit are the natural, supernatural result of walking in the spirit. And walking in the spirit is really very simple: Put God first place in your life, and make His Word your final authority. Spend time fellowshipping with Him every day in His Word and in prayer.

The moment you start doing those things, you'll automatically begin to change. Because you're giving God your time and attention, you'll begin rising above the lowlands of the flesh and ascending into a more supernatural lifestyle. As this starts happening, you'll begin thinking less like the world and more like your heavenly Father. You'll operate increasingly like Him as you outgrow your old carnal ways.

Simply reading this book will help you become more aware of the power of the fruit of the spirit. It will prepare your heart to receive from the Lord greater insight to help you come up higher in your spiritual walk. For example, learning what God's Word says about love will help strengthen and expand your love walk. Knowing what the Bible says about joy will make you more apt to rejoice. And as you set your mind on peace and decide to feed your faith with scriptures about patience and gentleness, those forces will flow more freely in your life.

How can I be sure that will happen?

You can be sure because it's a spiritual principle. Galatians 6 says:

> God is not mocked: for whatsoever a man soweth, that shall he also reap. For he that soweth to his flesh shall of the flesh reap corruption; but he that soweth to the Spirit shall of the Spirit reap life everlasting (verses 7-8).

Just as a farmer determines what kind of crop he's going to have by planting a certain kind of seed you, as a believer, determine what you're going to harvest in life by the spiritual seed you sow. God doesn't make the determination for you. He doesn't pick you out of the crowd and sovereignly decide to give you a bumper crop of good spiritual fruit. He leaves it up to you (Deuteronomy 30:19).

You can choose to either sow to the flesh by spending all your time and energy on carnal, worldly pursuits; or choose to sow to the spirit by investing in your relationship with God. Either way, you'll reap a return from the realm where you sow.

Some Christians don't understand this. They think they can sow to one place and receive a harvest from another. But that's not how things work. You can't spend all your time on the things of the flesh and live an abundant Spirit-filled life. It's not possible.

If you want to be able to respond supernaturally to the challenges you face each day, you have to make time in your daily schedule to fellowship with God in His Word and prayer.

If you want the forces of the spirit flowing out of you in such abundance that you can overcome tough situations when they arise, you have to keep your heart full of the Word. Otherwise, when things get rough, you'll just react in the natural. Your spirit will take a back seat and your flesh will take over.

"But Gloria," you might say, "if my flesh starts to take over, can't I grab my Bible and get myself straightened out again? Can't I take some time to pray and listen to some good faith-filled preaching and get back in the spirit?"

When trouble hits, you don't have the luxury of putting the situation on hold while you listen to a sermon about being an overcomer and try to figure out how to act. When something goes wrong, you often have to respond immediately. Depending on which realm you've been investing in, you automatically respond in the spirit or you react in the flesh.

I remember a testimony we aired on our daily television broadcast some years ago. It was shared by one of our Partners who'd been faced with a totally unexpected and unimaginable situation: His son was killed in an accident right before his eyes.

When it happened, the first thing that father thought of after realizing his son was dead was what the Bible says. He remembered the scriptures about Jesus raising Lazarus from the dead. He remembered that Mark 9:23 says, "All things are possible to him that believeth," and he acted accordingly. Right there, on the spot, he released his faith, declared the Word, and God raised his boy from the dead!

Had that father not been sowing to the spirit, he would have reacted in the flesh. When he saw his son in the jaws of death, he would have responded like any parent would in the natural. He would have started to weep and mourn and say, "My child is dead! What am I going to do?"

Because he'd been faithful to store up the Word in his heart, however, he had a reservoir of faith inside him. Because he'd been sowing to the spirit, in the time of crisis, his flesh took a back seat, his inner man took over, and he went beyond himself. The supernatural power of the Holy Spirit came to his aid and, at that critical moment, he and his son reaped life!

It Takes More Than Going to Church on Sunday

When you sow to your flesh, you go through life being naturally minded. You think about the things of the spirit only when you're facing catastrophe and you need God to bail you out. God is merciful, and He'll do that for you (often on the basis of someone else's prayers), but that's not how He wants you to live. He wants you to walk in the spirit every day, moment by moment, so that the supernatural becomes natural to you. He intends for you to be continually planting spiritual seed so you're constantly reaping abundant life.

Romans 8:6 says, "...to be spiritually minded is life and peace." So, the amount of time and attention you give to the Lord is how much life and peace will be multiplied back to you. If you give Him only an hour a week in church on Sunday, it will help you a little, but it won't produce the kind of sustained victory and fruitfulness Jesus has in mind for you. To experience that kind of life, you have to go after the things of the Spirit daily. You have to continue in the Word, and then as Jesus said, you will "know the truth, and the truth shall make you free" (John 8:31-32).

"But I have other responsibilities!" you might say. "I have other things in life I have to do. I can't spend all my time in church."

You don't have to! You're continuing in the Word every time you read your Bible and pray. You're continuing in the Word every time you tune in to a broadcast like *Believer's Voice of Victory* or listen to anointed preaching on the internet or other media resources. You're continuing in the Word every time you act on what God says—when you respond in love instead of selfishness, or forgive instead of being bitter, or do a good job at work instead of slacking off.

Speak Your Faith

I continue in the Word every day. I act on what God says. I respond in love instead of selfishness, I forgive instead of being bitter, and I do a good job at work and in whatever I set my hand to do. I walk in the spirit every day, moment by moment. I continue to plant spiritual seed, so I constantly reap abundant life!

All those things are part of continuing in the Word and, as you do them, your spirit becomes increasingly stronger. You're able to exercise dominion over your flesh and enjoy a greater abundance of life and peace because you're doing what God says.

I don't know if you've noticed, but when you do what God says, your life works. When you don't, it doesn't. When you act on what He says about love, for instance, your interactions with people will go more smoothly, and your relationships will become more gratifying and sweet. People will tend to respond well to you and want to be with you. And, they'll want to bless you.

When you get away from love and get into strife and unforgiveness, however, the opposite happens. Your relationships suffer. People don't want to be around you. They oppose you and make your life more difficult because the principle of sowing and reaping is always in operation. If you sow strife, that's what you'll get in return.

Of course, none of us have totally arrived when it comes to walking in the fruit of the spirit. We're all still developing in it, step by step. So, we're all in the process of learning and maturing. If we keep acting on all the light we have and searching for more light, that process will continue.

But if we let the natural affairs of life consume us, our progress will stop and the light on our pathway will start to go dim. Our flesh will take over again, and our inner man will begin to get weak and dry up.

Going Forward or Sliding Back?

I've found in my own life and in ministering to others that, spiritually, we're always either increasing or decreasing. We can't just coast along in neutral, maintaining the status quo by living on the Word we've stored up in the past. If we want our spirits to stay strong, we have to keep progressing in our walk with God. Otherwise, we'll start sliding backward and yielding to the flesh.

Why is that?

It's because this spiritually dark world around us is always trying to pull us in a fleshly direction. It's always endeavoring to entice us with some kind of sin. Think of all the ungodly things that come at us just through media, for example: advertisements featuring images intentionally designed to stir up fleshly lusts, movies filled with violence, foul language and people acting ugly toward each other. And, there are whole television programs that glamorize immoral behavior and treat it like it's normal.

These days, even the little situation comedies that air on TV during what was once called "the family hour" often portray sin as perfectly acceptable. They wrap funny stories around things like fornication and adultery and send the message: *There's nothing wrong with having sex outside of marriage. It's OK. You just have to use your best judgment and be safe about it.*

That message is a total lie! God says it's wrong to have sex outside of marriage, and that means it is. It's a violation of His plan, and if you do it, it will bring harm to you. It will put you in bondage to the flesh and to the devil.

The culture of this world will try to make you forget about that. It will do its best to convince you that you'll be freer if you forget about what God says in the Bible. It will tell you you'll be happier and more fulfilled if you'll just yield to your fleshly desires and do whatever you want.

That's why it's so important to spend time every day with the Lord, reading His Word and hearing from Him. Not only is His input vital to your spiritual growth, you need the continual inflow of strength that comes from hearing what He says and seeing life the way He sees it. You need the clarity that comes when you follow these instructions in Romans 12:

> I beseech you therefore, brethren, by the mercies of God, that ye present your bodies a living sacrifice, holy, acceptable unto God, which is your reasonable service. And be not conformed to this world: but be ye transformed by the renewing of your mind, that ye may prove [discern] what is that good, and acceptable, and perfect, will of God (verses 1-2).

When you're constantly in the process of renewing your mind with the Word, the world can't force you into its mold. It can't pressure you into conforming to its influence because the truth of the Word will counter that influence. It will keep your spirit strong so that, even in the midst of a sin-darkened culture, you can keep walking in the light.

You'll still face some problems in life, of course. That's just a part of living on planet Earth. But as long as you stay in the Word, you'll have an answer to those problems. The Lord will tell you what to do in the midst of them and move supernaturally in your behalf to help you.

His nature inside you is as eternal and boundless as He is. So if you keep giving Him first place in your life, developing and progressing in all the fruit of the spirit, you can go as far with God as you want to go!

There's no limit to the amount of victory and blessing you can experience if you'll keep moving forward in the Word and in fellowship with God!

The reason so many Christians seem to be stuck where they are and can't seem to overcome their fleshly habits and sins, is often because they don't understand the spiritual principle of sowing and reaping. They don't know they need to keep cultivating the forces in their inner man. They may want to go on with God to higher places and strive to live a more victorious Christian life, but they don't plant the seeds that will produce such victory. They don't strengthen their spirits by setting their attention on God.

As a result, their flesh keeps bossing them around, and they eventually become discouraged. "I just can't do this!" they say. "I want to live right and please the Lord, but it seems I'm not able to do it. I might as well just stop trying and give up!"

Out of Your Heart Are the Outgoings of Life

Ken felt that way not long after he was born again, when he was trying to quit smoking. He became frustrated and felt condemned because no matter how hard he tried, he repeatedly failed.

In his heart, he so desperately wanted to kick the habit that sometimes, in a fresh burst of determination, he'd throw his cigarettes out the car window while he was driving down the road. Then a few minutes later, he'd have second thoughts and go back and hunt around alongside the highway, looking for the pack he threw away. He felt bad about it, but he just couldn't seem to help himself!

Eventually, however, Ken got his attention off the smoking problem and just got caught up in the Word. He started spending every free moment reading his Bible, praying and listening to good, anointed preaching.

He even accepted an invitation to sing for a series of believers' meetings that were being held in Houston.

During the two weeks of those meetings, he attended services literally night and day. He was so busy, he didn't really have much time to smoke, so he left his cigarettes in the car. After the last meeting was over, he got in the car to drive back home and saw his pack of cigarettes tucked up above the sun visor. *I haven't smoked in two weeks and I haven't even missed it,* he thought. *I'm sure not going to go back to it now.* So he threw those cigarettes away and never smoked again.

What made the difference? ***He'd been sowing to the spirit!*** He'd been setting his mind on God and saturating himself in the Word, and the Word separated him from the cravings of his flesh. It weakened his desire for tobacco and strengthened his spirit so that what had previously been impossible for him became relatively easy.

The same kind of thing can happen to you!

It doesn't matter what kind of problem you've had with your flesh or how long you've struggled with it, if you'll keep sowing to the spirit, you'll reap a harvest of victory. If you continue in the Word and set your mind on the things of God, that flesh problem you've been struggling with will drop away.

It might not disappear overnight. It might try to hang on for a little while. But eventually, because you're putting God first in your life, your spirit will take dominion. God's image in your inner man will shine through to your outer man. The fruit of the spirit will spring forth from your heart, and you'll overcome whatever it is that's been giving you trouble.

I must warn you, though: While you're pressing toward your break-through, the devil will do his best to distract you. He'll try to get you so busy with the natural affairs of life that you stop focusing on the Word. He'll use "the cares of this world, and the deceitfulness of riches, and the lusts of other things" to choke the Word out of your heart and make it unfruitful (Mark 4:19).

As Jesus taught in the parable of the sower, this is one of Satan's primary strategies. So stay alert, and don't be duped by him! Regardless of what he does, choose to keep your attention on God and do what He commanded in Proverbs 4:

> My son, attend to my words; incline thine ear unto my sayings. Let them not depart from thine eyes; keep them in the midst of thine heart. For they are life unto those that find them, and health to all their flesh. Keep thy heart with all diligence; for out of it are the issues of life (verses 20-23).

The word *issues* in that passage literally means "outgoings" or "outflowings." It refers to the fruit or forces of the spirit that bring the goodness of God into manifestation in your life. They push out of your life the contamination of the world and the devil, and deliver you from anything that isn't from God.

When you fill your heart with the Word, the forces of the spirit flow out from your inner man and oppose everything that's contrary to you.

One time, Ken and I were ministering in the Philippines, and I was studying in the hotel room, preparing to teach from Proverbs 4. When I looked out the window, I noticed a beautiful fountain shooting water high into the air. As I watched, I realized that as long as the fountain was overflowing to any degree at all, no trash could stay in it. The force of the water coming out of the mouth of the fountain would push the trash out.

As I thought about that, the Lord showed me our hearts are like the mouth of that fountain. It's the place from which the spiritual forces of God spring forth. As long as we keep our hearts centered on God and filled with His Word, those spiritual forces keep flowing. They continually pour out of us and keep us free from the trash of this world.

It's no wonder the Bible says to "keep and guard your heart with all vigilance and above all that you guard" (verse 23, AMPC). Your heart should be the primary focus of your life. It determines whether you live in victory or defeat.

Whatever you're walking in today is a result of what you put in your heart yesterday. What you walk in tomorrow will be a result of what you put in it today. Your future is literally stored up in your heart!

Keep Abiding in the Vine

Jesus said, "A good man out of the good treasure of the heart bringeth forth good things: and an evil man out of the evil treasure bringeth forth evil things" (Matthew 12:35). In other words, whatever is in your heart is going to come out, so if you want your outcome to be good, you can't afford to be a lazy Christian. You can't devote all your time to the things of the natural and expect that somehow, magically, your life will overflow with the treasure of God.

If you want to enjoy a life filled with good treasure and supernatural blessing, you have to make time every day to "seek those things which are above" (Colossians 3:1). Diligently store up God's Word in your heart, and keep developing your relationship with Him.

As believers, we ought to go about our day so tuned in to the Lord that He can get our attention anytime He wants it. We should strive to stay in touch with Him moment by moment so we can always hear what He's saying on the inside of us. Then, when He prompts us to take a different route to work to avoid an accident or leads us to pray for someone in the grocery store, we can be quick to obey. When He tells us to do something, we'll be sensitive and ready to respond.

There's nothing more important to our lives and well-being than keeping our hearts in touch with the Lord. There's nothing more vital than maintaining a living connection with Him. The stronger our union with Him, the more effortlessly and abundantly we bear the fruit of the spirit.

As Jesus said in John 15:

> I am the True Vine, and My Father is the Vinedresser. Any branch in Me that does not bear fruit [that stops bearing] He cuts away (trims off, takes away); and He cleanses and repeatedly prunes every branch that continues to bear fruit, to make it bear more and richer and more excellent fruit. You are cleansed and pruned already, because of the word which I have given you [the teachings I have discussed with you]. Dwell in Me, and I will dwell in you. [Live in Me, and I will live in you.] Just as no branch can bear fruit of itself without abiding in (being vitally united to) the vine, neither can you bear fruit unless you abide in Me. I am the Vine; you are the branches. Whoever lives in Me and I in him bears much (abundant) fruit. However, apart from Me [cut off from vital union with Me] you can do nothing.... If you live in Me [abide vitally united to Me] and My words remain in you and continue to live in your hearts, ask whatever you will, and it shall be done for you. When you bear (produce) much fruit, My Father is honored and glorified, and you show and prove yourselves to be true followers of Mine (verses 1-5, 7-8, AMPC).

Notice, according to those verses, the Word of God has a tremendous impact on our ability to walk in the spirit. It cleanses us from the nonproductive things in our lives and enables us to be more fruitful. It prunes away fleshly hindrances so that we can be more blessed and free. It enables us to receive answers to our prayers.

I'm telling you, the Word of God is wonderful! It's not just a book of facts and information. It's supernatural! It's "alive and full of power...active, operative, energizing, and effective" (Hebrews 4:12, AMPC).

When we really take heed to God's Word and commune with Him over it, expecting to receive revelation, the Word causes good things to happen in us. (As Ken and I like to say: **"Just one word from God can change your life forever!"**)

If, on the other hand, we don't take the time to feed on the Word, we won't be able to connect with the power of God that's within it.

We'll be like that branch Jesus talked about that is separated from the vine. No matter how close together a vine and a branch might be, if there's not a living connection between the two, the life of the vine can't flow into the branch. And without that life, the branch can't bear fruit. It just withers and dries up.

That's the picture Jesus was painting when He said, "Apart from me you can do nothing" (John 15:5, NLT). He was saying, "If you don't take time to nurture your connection with Me and My Word, you're not going to produce any signs of spiritual life. Even though the Father loves you and wants to bless you, you'll so limit Him in what He can do for you that you'll end up living just like the people down the street who don't know Him at all."

Personally, I've decided I'm never going to let myself get into that condition. I've made up my mind I'm going to tend to my union with the Lord and attend diligently to His Word so that I can continually bear "much abundant fruit."

Since you're reading this book, I'm confident you've made the same decision. You've set your heart on things above and made a commitment to sow to the spirit. You've determined to invest in your relationship with God. As you study each chapter, release your faith to receive a return on that investment. Believe that as you set your attention on what the

Scriptures say about the fruit of the spirit, you're going to reap a harvest of that fruit in your life.

Believe, too, that you're going to hear personally from the Holy Spirit. And as you're reading the words on these pages, pay attention to what you're hearing in your heart. The Holy Spirit lives there, and that's where He communicates with you. So tune in to Him, and let Him empower, encourage and correct you, as only He can.

If you've been through a dry spiritual season in your life and you haven't been living for God for a while, don't be discouraged about it. Don't let the devil condemn you and tell you that you've gotten so far away from God you can never get back. That's not true! You can get back to God in a moment.

No matter what you've done or how badly you may have messed up, if you've been born again you're still God's child. You still have a new man inside you and a new heart that's created in God's likeness. You still have His life and the fruit of His spirit within you. So just repent and receive His forgiveness.

Speak Your Faith

Heavenly Father, I'm returning to You, and I'm going to follow You. I'm going to make You and Your Word my first priority and final authority. Teach me what I need to know, and help me to increasingly walk in the spirit with You.

Are you ready to get started?

Then let's find out what the Word of God says about love!

Chapter 4

THE GREATEST OF THESE IS LOVE

*But earnestly desire and zealously cultivate the greatest
and best gifts and graces (the higher gifts and the choicest
graces). And yet I will show you a still more excellent way
[one that is better by far and the highest of them all—love].*

1 CORINTHIANS 12:31, AMPC

Christians have many different ideas about what it means to be "spiritual." Some think it means being a little strange or otherworldly. Others equate it with having spectacular experiences with God, being gifted to work miracles, signs and wonders, or being especially devoted to church work.

The Scriptures, however, describe what it means to be a spiritual person in another way altogether. They sum it up in a single word: *love.*

According to the New Testament, a truly spiritual believer is love-ruled, yielded to and giving expression to God, who "is love" (1 John 4:8).

Love is the greatest manifestation of spirituality there is! (See 1 Corinthians 13:13.) It heads the list of all the fruit of the spirit. When love is present in a person's life, every other fruit is present, as well. Love is the foundation and moving principle behind them all. As Alexander Maclaren wrote about the fruit of love: "It is the life sap which rises through the tree and gives form to all the clusters."[2]

Love holds the other fruit together and causes them to all function together in perfect unity (Colossians 3:14, NIV). Produced in the heart of the believer by the Holy Spirit, the divine force of love is unfailingly powerful. Unlike the feeble, natural kind of love the world offers, it isn't tainted and weakened by selfishness. Its primary ingredient is self-sacrifice for the benefit of the one loved. Donald Gee calls it "the love that God is," because it is, quite literally, God's own love.

God's love is not self-seeking, it's self-giving. It's all-encompassing and unconditional. It remains constant regardless of whether or not it receives a response.

God so loved the world that even after mankind rebelled against Him and rejected Him, "He gave his only begotten Son, that whosoever believeth in him should not perish, but have everlasting life" (John 3:16).

Natural, human love can hardly grasp such a thing! It can hardly imagine dying even for someone who is especially good. "But God demonstrates His own love toward us, in that while we were still sinners, Christ died for us" (Romans 5:8, NKJV).

That's how great the love of God is!

"But Gloria," you might say, "I can't love like God does!"

Yes, you can. As a born-again believer, you have His nature. Just as God is Love, you are love. Therefore, His love is your natural, supernatural disposition.

---

2 Alexander Maclaren, "Galatians: The Fruit of the Spirit," in *Expositions of Holy Scripture: 2 Corinthians, Galatians and Philippians Chapters 1 to End. Colossians, Thessalonians, and 1 Timothy* (New York: Scriptura Press, 1910, 2015).

You may not be acting like it right now. Your flesh may not feel very loving at times. But if you've made Jesus Christ the Lord of your life, "the love of God is shed abroad" in your heart by the Holy Ghost (Romans 5:5). It is there in your spirit, regardless of how you may or may not be feeling, and your No. 1 calling as a believer is to let it flow out.

Clearly, if we want to enjoy God's manifested blessings, we must keep love at the forefront of our thinking.

As the Apostle Paul wrote:

> If I [can] speak in the tongues of men and [even] of angels, but have not love (that reasoning, intentional, spiritual devotion such as is inspired by God's love for and in us), I am only a noisy gong or a clanging cymbal. And if I have prophetic powers (the gift of interpreting the divine will and purpose), and understand all the secret truths and mysteries and possess all knowledge, and if I have [sufficient] faith so that I can remove mountains, but have not love (God's love in me) I am nothing (a useless nobody). Even if I dole out all that I have [to the poor in providing] food, and if I surrender my body to be burned or in order that I may glory, but have not love (God's love in me), I gain nothing (1 Corinthians 13:1-3, AMPC).

Love is the bottom line! Nothing counts without it. When God's love isn't being expressed in our lives, speaking in tongues is just noise, and being able to prophesy and move mountains with our faith doesn't mean anything. Apart from love, even our giving doesn't matter.

If we want to better our lives physically, mentally, spiritually, financially and socially, we'll have to start by getting our love lives straight.

Not Yet Picture-Perfect? Make a Change!

What exactly does walking in love look like?

Paul gives us a perfect picture in the remainder of 1 Corinthians 13:

> Love endures long and is patient and kind; love never is envious
> nor boils over with jealousy, is not boastful or vainglorious,
> does not display itself haughtily. It is not conceited (arrogant
> and inflated with pride); it is not rude (unmannerly) and does
> not act unbecomingly. Love (God's love in us) does not insist
> on its own rights or its own way, for it is not self-seeking; it is
> not touchy or fretful or resentful; it takes no account of the
> evil done to it [it pays no attention to a suffered wrong]. It
> does not rejoice at injustice and unrighteousness, but rejoices
> when right and truth prevail. Love bears up under anything
> and everything that comes, is ever ready to believe the best of
> every person, its hopes are fadeless under all circumstances,
> and it endures everything [without weakening]. Love never
> fails... (verses 4-8, AMPC).

In my own life, when I want to focus more on my love walk, I read
those verses daily and insert my name into them. I turn them into confessions of faith and apply each one of them to myself. Instead of saying,
"Love endures long and is patient and kind..." I say, "Gloria endures long
and is patient and kind," etc.

As I go through each verse, I check up on myself in that area. If I see
that rather than being patient I've been short-tempered with someone, I'll
acknowledge I've missed it. I'll repent and make a change there.

Making changes is a continual part of walking in love, not just for
me, but for us all. Due to the influence of the world and the devil, we all
have unloving habits and attitudes to overcome. If we didn't grow up in a
godly home with parents who knew the Word, those habits might even

have been purposely instilled in us. We might actually have been raised to be selfish, to carry grudges, take revenge when wronged, or to be critical of other people.

If you came from that kind of background, such things might have been considered so normal in your home that, as an unbeliever, you did them without noticing. But now that you've received Jesus as Lord, things are different. You have the Holy Spirit inside you to bring those things to your attention.

As you renew your mind to the ways of love by spending time in the Word, you start noticing where you're out of line in your love walk, and you're able to change.

That's how it was for me. I began my Christian life as an adult. I had to start from scratch learning about the God kind of love because I hadn't been taught about it as a child. Because Ken and I were both born again before we started having children, however, in *our* home it's been a different story. Our children are grown and have their own families now, but we started teaching them about God's love when they were just toddlers.

If you're a parent with young children, I recommend you do the same. Take the time to read the Bible and talk to your children about how important it is to be loving. Live God's love in front of them. Show them by example how to live unselfishly and to let love rule in their hearts.

Speak Your Faith

I endure long, and I'm patient and kind. I am never envious, nor do I boil over with jealousy. I am not boastful or vainglorious, and I do not display myself haughtily. I am not conceited (arrogant and inflated with pride). I am not rude (unmannerly), and I do not act unbecomingly. I do not insist on my own rights or my own way, for I am not self-seeking. I am not touchy or fretful or resentful. I take no account of the evil done to me [I pay no attention to a suffered wrong]. I do not rejoice at injustice and unrighteousness, but I rejoice when right and truth prevail. I bear up under anything and everything that comes, I am ever ready to believe the best of every person. My hopes are fadeless under all circumstances, and I endure everything [without weakening]. I never fail because God's love in me never fades out or becomes obsolete or comes to an end!

Take a Love Checkup

I can tell you from experience, it's wonderful to live in a home where love rules! It's like living in a little slice of heaven on earth. Even if you're the only love-ruled person in your family, you can sweeten the atmosphere around you. You can make a major difference—not only at home but at the office, at school or anywhere else you go—just by walking in love.

Let's look again at each verse in 1 Corinthians 13:4-8, AMPC, and you'll see why:

"Love endures long and is patient and kind." When you're walking in love, you don't get snippy and irritated with people who aren't acting the way you want them to. You treat them kindly, and instead of getting exasperated with them, you're longsuffering because love doesn't wear out. It doesn't give up on people.

Even if it's wronged repeatedly, love forgives "seventy times seven" (Matthew 18:22). It overflows with so much mercy that its mercies are "new every morning" (Lamentations 3:23). Whatever it takes, love keeps seeking opportunities to do good things for others and to be a blessing to them.

"Love never is envious nor boils over with jealousy." When you're walking in love, you celebrate with people and share their joy when they receive a blessing or experience success. You don't resent them for getting the car, the house or the promotion you wanted. If Satan tempts you to do so, you respond like my daughter, Kellie, did one time when she was about 3 years old. Her room was a mess and Ken said to her, "Kellie, you get in there and pick up those toys." She answered him right back and said, "That's not my thought!"

That's how love talks to the devil. When he comes around you with his ugly ideas and attitudes, love rises up in you and rebukes him: "No, Devil. That's not my thought! I'm not taking that envy. I'm not taking that jealousy. I'm walking in love."

"[Love] is not boastful or vainglorious, does not display itself haughtily. It is not conceited (arrogant and inflated with pride)." Love doesn't puff you up and cause you to act like you're a big shot. It moves you to lift up other people. Rather than making you want to show off to everyone how wonderful you are, love causes you to focus on those around you. It makes you want them to know how wonderful *they* are!

"[Love] is not rude (unmannerly) and does not act unbecomingly." Love will cause you to be courteous even when other people are behaving rudely toward you. It will empower you to hold your tongue and respond in every situation in a way that reflects the nature of God. When the waiter in the restaurant doesn't give you the proper attention, for example, love will inspire you to be nice to him anyway. Love will cause you to extend grace to him and bless him with a good tip!

"Love...does not insist on its own rights or its own way, for it is not self-seeking." This characteristic of love can save your marriage. It will stop hurtful arguments before they start. When a disagreement arises between you and your spouse, if you'll put the other person's desires before your

own instead of insisting on getting your own way, you'll have peace instead of turmoil in your home.

"But I'm not the one who's in the wrong at our house," you might say. "My spouse is the one who needs to change!"

That may be so, but someone has to take the first step. Someone has to stop saying, "I have a right to do this! I have a right to have that!" *You* be the one who makes the change. Speak words of love instead of selfishness, and you'll open the door for God to work.

"[Love] is not touchy or fretful or resentful." Sometimes, we have trouble not being fretful when someone hurts our feelings. I've had to remind myself a lot over the years that "I am not touchy, fretful or resentful." Some of my friends have, too.

One friend, for instance, used to get upset with her husband because he always forgot her birthday. He did it every year, and every time she reacted the same way: She went around the house all day fuming about it. She slammed the cabinet doors and banged the pots and pans around. In spite of it all, however, nothing changed. Her husband didn't even notice anything was wrong. He wasn't bothered at all by her resentment. She was the only one who was hurt by it. By choosing to be so touchy, she ruined her whole day.

Eventually, however, she caught hold of the revelation in 1 Corinthians 13. She realized that "love takes no account of the evil done to it [it pays no attention to a suffered wrong]." So, she gave up her resentment and just began reminding her husband about her birthdays. After that, her birthdays were a lot more fun!

Just think how much trouble you could avoid if you followed her example. Think how much more enjoyable life would be if every time someone hurt your feelings or slighted you in some way, instead of letting it ruin your day and make you depressed, you said to yourself, "I take no account of a suffered wrong." What would happen? You'd go free. That offense would lose its ability to hurt you.

Any way you look at it, that's a good deal. So, take it! Don't keep a little book in your mind where you write down every bad thing someone does to you. Close the book on those things, and throw it away. Let those offenses go, and forgive the people who committed them. Otherwise, those offenses will keep hurting *you*.

What's worse, they'll do damage to your family. I've seen it happen. I've seen family feuds handed down from generation to generation and resentments that have lasted so long no one can even remember what triggered them. I've seen conflicts between people that persist, keeping the door open, year after year, to the devil's attacks.

You don't want to bring that kind of trash into your home! You don't want your children to grow up thinking retribution and treating other people as enemies is a way of life. Even if you had a hard background yourself, you don't want to pass it along and perpetuate attitudes of unforgiveness. So break that family curse right now, in the Name of Jesus!

Unforgiveness is one of the worst enemies you can have. It's the opposite of love, and it will hurt you. It will make your body sick and paralyze your faith. That's the reason Jesus said when He taught on faith in Mark 11:25, "When ye stand praying, forgive, if ye have ought against any." Unforgiveness stops the prayer of faith from working. It shuts the door on God and keeps Him from being able to move in your situation.

Love, on the other hand, does just the reverse. It causes your faith to function effectively because, as Galatians 5:6 says, "Faith...worketh by love"!

"Love bears up under anything and everything that comes, is ever ready to believe the best of every person, its hopes are fadeless under all circumstances, and it endures everything [without weakening]. Love never fails." The devil may try to tell you that walking in love toward people who do

you wrong is a sign of weakness, but actually it's the ultimate sign of strength.

Love is the most powerful of all the fruit of the spirit. It will enable you to respond in a godly way to any situation. It will give you the strength to control yourself so completely that contrary people and circumstances won't even be able to shake you, much less bring you down.

Love opens the door wide for God to move in your life. It paves the way for Him to answer your prayers.

Put the Past Behind You, and Make a New Choice

"Well," you might say, "love may not ever fail, but there sure have been times in my life when I've failed to walk in it!"

That's been true of all of us at times. But you don't have to stay in that place of failure. You can repent and receive God's forgiveness. You can put the past behind you.

Even if you've spent years living in selfishness, strife and unforgiveness, you don't have to continue in that unloving lifestyle. You can choose to change. If you're born again, love is your new nature, and you have the power and ability to walk in it. Sin has lost its dominion over you. The old man you used to be has died and gone, so you can choose not to let selfishness rule over you anymore. You can start yielding to your reborn spirit and allowing the forces in your new inward nature to flow out daily.

So make the choice. You're not going to just wake up one morning and find that, without any effort on your part, all selfishness has left you and you're just dripping with the love of God. That's not going to happen! At some point, you have to make a quality decision to choose love. Then, once you've made that decision, you have to stick with it. Keep choosing, in each new situation, to yield to love and resist the fleshly impulses that are contrary to it.

Speak Your Faith

I choose to live in the love of God. I'm going to be love-ruled today. I choose to yield to the fruit of the spirit today. I yield to love, joy, peace, patience, goodness, kindness, faithfulness, gentleness and self-control!

I start every day by making that choice. During my daily prayer time, I speak the words we just spoke together out loud. Since I have my prayer time first thing in the morning, that means before I ever come into contact with anyone else, I've already made my commitment to let the forces of the spirit flow out of me. I've already set myself up to have a good day.

I don't like to have any bad days! I'm sure you don't either, so I encourage you to make applying 1 Corinthians 13 a part of your morning routine. Don't wait until you're halfway through your day and you've already gotten mad about something, to remember what the Bible says about love. Remind yourself of it every morning when you first get up.

If you want to strengthen your love life even more, tuck a mini-sized New Testament into your pocket or purse so you can keep 1 Corinthians 13:4-8 handy throughout the day. Write down verses about love and tape them to your mirror where you can look at them at night while you're getting ready for bed. Put another copy on your refrigerator. (That way you'll see it a lot!) Read and confess the love scriptures over yourself often, so you can keep them at the forefront of your mind. As you do those things, love will begin to be a habit. It will take over your life, and you'll start to walk in it without having to think about it.

You'll still miss it at times, of course. We're all still growing in these things. But as the Word becomes integrated into your spirit, the moment you step out of the love walk, that Word will rise up in your heart and correct you. When it does, be honest and say, "Lord, thank You for showing me that! I was wrong. I repent, and I receive Your forgiveness. Help me to make a change there. Help me to be kinder to that person, and to be patient in this situation."

That's a prayer you can be sure will be answered! You already have the Helper, the Holy Spirit, living inside you, and His primary mission is to help you do God's will. So, the moment you express your desire to yield to the force of love, He'll enable you to do it. He'll come immediately to your aid. Then you can go on about your day being a blessing to the people around you and having a wonderful time yourself!

Living Contact Keeps It Flowing

Am I saying that choosing the lifestyle of love will always be easy? No.

Even though you have a fountain of love springing up in your spirit, and you have the Holy Spirit to help you, you'll still go through some tests and trials. The devil will see to that! He'll always be trying to use contrary people and difficult situations to pull you off course.

You don't have to let him succeed, though. You can always overcome his attacks because he can only try to influence you with what you can feel and see. He can only use carnal thoughts and imaginations to tempt you to get out of love and into disobedience.

But you're not limited to the natural realm. You have weapons of spiritual warfare that are "not carnal, but mighty through God to the pulling down of strong holds;) casting down imaginations, and every high thing that exalteth itself against the knowledge of God" (2 Corinthians 10:4-5).

You also have the assurance that "there hath no temptation taken you but such as is common to man: but God is faithful, who will not suffer you to be tempted above that ye are able; but will with the temptation also make a way to escape" (1 Corinthians 10:13).

You have every advantage over the devil! You can deal with and overcome anything he throws at you. All you have to do is stand on God's Word, and let the supernatural forces of the spirit flow out of you. Those spiritual forces will keep you from being pulled over into the natural and enticed to sin. They'll hold you steady so that instead of wavering in the face of temptation, your love walk will remain consistent.

Think about how consistent God is. He never changes (Malachi 3:6; Hebrews 13:8). In Him there is no "variableness, neither shadow of turning" (James 1:17), so there doesn't have to be any in you, either. You have the forces of His Spirit inside you, and you can let them flow through you to give you victory in every test and trial—every day!

The way you keep those forces flowing, as I've said before, is by staying in living contact with God, spending time with Him in the Word and in prayer. Draw near to Him in praise and worship. As you strengthen your connection with Him, your revelation of His love for you will keep increasing and, as a result, your love for Him will grow.

God's love for you, and your love for Him, will motivate you to break the power of selfishness in your life and make you want to please Him. As you spend time with Him, you'll conform more to the image of Jesus. Just like He did, you'll love other people—even when they're acting unlovely.

The more you fellowship with the Father, the more you look like the Son!

The more you feed on His written Word, which is infused with His life and the forces of His Spirit, the more His love will pour out of you. As Romans 13:8 says, "He that loveth another hath fulfilled the law." So ultimately, your living contact with God will result in your keeping *all* His commandments! You'll wind up not striving to obey a set of rules but simply receiving His love and letting it flow through you toward others.

Jesus taught this, time and again, in the Gospels. He said:

> If ye love me, keep my commandments.... He that hath my commandments, and keepeth them, he it is that loveth me: and he that loveth me shall be loved of my Father, and I will love him, and will manifest myself to him (John 14:15, 21).

> If a man love me, he will keep my words: and my Father will love him, and we will come unto him, and make our abode with him (verse 23).

> If ye abide in me, and my words abide in you, ye shall ask what ye will, and it shall be done unto you. Herein is my Father glorified, that ye bear much fruit; so shall ye be my disciples (John 15:7-8).

> If ye keep my commandments, ye shall abide in my love; even as I have kept my Father's commandments, and abide in his love.... This is my commandment, That ye love one another, as I have loved you (verses 10, 12).

Notice, Jesus didn't refer to love as an option in those verses. He called it our *commandment*. That means when we're not walking in love, we're in disobedience.

Disobedience is dangerous! Just as when we obey God's Word we experience victory and live as overcomers, when we disobey Him, we experience defeat. We step out of the light and start stumbling around in darkness. That's not a safe thing to do. We want to stay protected and on the victory side. We want to walk continually in God's power and manifested presence by communing with Him in His Word and keeping His command of love. As 1 John says:

> Whoso keepeth his word, in him verily is the love of God perfected (1 John 2:5).

He that loveth his brother abideth in the light, and there is none occasion of stumbling in him (verse 10).

God is love; and he that dwelleth in love dwelleth in God, and God in him (1 John 4:16).

For this is the love of God, that we keep his commandments: and his commandments are not grievous. For whatsoever is born of God overcometh the world: and this is the victory that overcometh the world, even our faith (1 John 5:3-4).

"Go in Love, and I Shall Always Be With Thee"

In addition to spending time in the Word, another way you can strengthen your living connection with God is by praying in other tongues. That's a wonderful way to fellowship with Him. It enables you to communicate with Him freely, right out of your spirit. When you're praying in tongues, because you're not limited to just praying about what you know, you can pray beyond your understanding. You can speak mysteries and give thanks directly from your heart (1 Corinthians 14:2, 17).

Does that affect your love life?

Certainly, it does. Jude 20-21 connects praying in tongues and love: "You, beloved, building yourselves up on your most holy faith, praying in the Holy Spirit, keep yourselves in the love of God" (NKJV).

Keeping yourself in the love of God is the key to everything when it comes to living a victorious Christian life! It enables you to walk in all the other forces of the spirit, and keeps the door open for them to continue to flow.

Speak Your Faith

I keep God's Word and the love of God is perfected in me. I love others, and I abide in the light. There is no occasion of stumbling in me. God is Love. I dwell in Him, and He dwells in me. I keep His commandments, and His commandments are not grievous (burdensome or oppressive). I am born of God, and I overcome the world. This is the victory that overcomes the world, even my faith!

Without love, you'll never be able to walk in joy because you'll be too self-centered. You'll get upset every time something doesn't go your way, or someone doesn't treat you right. Joy is totally dependent on your love life.

When you're walking in love, you can keep rejoicing no matter what happens. If someone wrongs you, you don't have to come down to Satan's level and wrong that person in return. Instead, you can be kind to those who oppose you. You can trust God to take care of you and do what Jesus said in Matthew 5:44: "Love your enemies, bless them that curse you, do good to them that hate you, and pray for them which despitefully use you."

When you do that, you position yourself to receive God's supernatural protection and deliverance. You're able to ask Him for the help you need and be certain He'll answer. Why? Because as 1 John 3:21-23 says:

> Beloved, if our heart condemn us not, then have we confidence toward God. And whatsoever we ask, we receive of him, because we keep his commandments, and do those things that are pleasing in his sight. And this is his commandment, That we should believe on the name of his Son Jesus Christ, and love one another, as he gave us commandment.

Really, when you walk in the love of God, you're the one who benefits the most. His love is so powerful and strong, it will enable you to overcome in any situation. It will make you more than a conqueror in every area of life by keeping you in constant contact with God.

Rufus Mosely wrote about this in his book *Manifest Victory*.[3] He tells about a time in his life when he'd been reading John 15 and wondering what Jesus meant in John 15:4 when He said, "Abide in me." He was eager to obey that command but he thought, *How can I do that? How can I abide in living contact with Jesus, all the time, every day?*

He prayed and asked the Lord about it, and the Lord said to him, *My presence shall go with thee and give thee rest. Go in love, and I shall always be with thee.*[4]

Those simple words changed Rufus Mosely's life. He said:

> I knew this was the secret! If we abide in God's love and always go in love, feeling and willing and giving out nothing but love and all possible love to all men and all things, we will always be in Him and under His anointing....
>
> It was made known to me that I could write editorials and do everything else that can be done in the loving Spirit of Jesus. I could even be in Heavenly places while plowing with a mule, pruning trees, in courtrooms and death cells, in all places of need, provided all was done in the Spirit of love....
>
> I was made glad and free almost beyond belief. God had simplified everything to me and made sure that heaven can and will be everywhere as we go in His love, manifesting His love and nothing but His love. The master key of the

---

3   J.R. Moseley, *Manifest Victory* (Saint Paul: Macalester Park Publishing Company, 1986) p. 117.
4   Ibid., 117.

Kingdom of Heaven, of abiding union with Jesus had been given me....[5]

Your only responsibility is the responsibility of being in union with Me....[6] Love is the condition and the bond of the union with Jesus.... If you love, you have everything. If you miss love, you miss everything. For in God love is everything.[7]

This one revelation makes our lives as believers "gloriously easy," Rufus Mosely realized. We can simply enter into union with Jesus, yield to His Spirit, and give out His love all the time. The more we do that, the more we overflow with His victory and glory. The more our motive in life is to love people, the more we win them to the Lord and His way of life, and the more successful we become in all our practical affairs. "If you're giving out God's love all the time, you will be in God all the time, for you are always a part of what you are giving out."[8]

What Are You Famous For?

This is the way evangelism is supposed to work. We're to draw people to Jesus by our love!

Love is what everyone wants, but they can't find it out there in the world because the world operates in selfishness. It says, "You have to look out for No. 1. You have to look out for yourself first because no one else will."

The love of God, on the other hand, looks out for the other person. So, when you're walking in His love, people notice. They respond. They see in you what they've been hungering for. Love opens the door of their hearts, and they're drawn to you.

---

5   Ibid., 117.
6   Ibid., 121.
7   Ibid., 133.
8   Ibid., 122.

God's love in us makes us shine as bright lights in a dark world.

As Jesus said in John 13:35, we're to be known by all men for our love. Although that's God's plan, we've often fallen short of it. We've yielded to our flesh, and instead of giving people God's love, we've just offered them a form of religion.

Religion gives people a set of rules and regulations. It tells them, "If you do these certain things, and you don't do those other things, you'll be in good standing with our group." That's not the message of Christianity! Christianity is not a religion. It's the Father and His family. It's living in fellowship with Him, receiving His love, and giving it out to others.

Jesus was the first Man to ever do that. He left heaven, came to earth and took upon Himself flesh. He revealed to the world, for the first time, what God's unconditional love is really like. He walked among the people and showed them mercy and kindness. He cared for them and "went about doing good, and healing all that were oppressed of the devil" (Acts 10:38).

That's exactly what the Church is supposed to be doing with the love of God today. We should be walking in love and blessing people at every opportunity. We should be doing good and making it easier for people to know that God is Love.

It's hard for them to have confidence in Him when they see Christians acting mean and ugly and fussing with each other. They look at us and think, *If that's Christianity, I'm not interested.* When they see us being kind and helpful, on the other hand, they respond more positively. When they see us taking every opportunity to serve them, they're likely to say, "I want to know the God that person is always talking about. I want what they have."

Just think, someone's salvation could depend on your love life!

"No one's salvation depends on me," you might say. "I'm not the Savior. Jesus is!"

Yes, but as Christians, we're Jesus' representatives in the world. What people see in us, they equate with Him. So, to a great degree, His reputation depends on us.

That's the reason He commands us to walk in love! That's why Paul prayed in Ephesians 3:14-19:

> For this cause I bow my knees unto the Father of our Lord Jesus Christ, of whom the whole family in heaven and earth is named, that he would grant you, according to the riches of his glory, to be strengthened with might by his Spirit in the inner man; that Christ may dwell in your hearts by faith; that ye, being rooted and grounded in love, may be able to comprehend with all saints what is the breadth, and length, and depth, and height; and to know the love of Christ, which passeth knowledge, that ye might be filled with all the fulness of God.

In the AMPC, the last verse of that passage has even more impact. It says that you can receive such a revelation of God's love that you can "be filled [through all your being] unto all the fullness of God [...have the richest measure of the divine Presence, and become a body wholly filled and flooded with God Himself]!"

Talk about a wonderful way to live! How would we as believers act if we knew we were filled with the richest measure of God's presence? What would we do if we were wholly flooded with Love Himself?

I can tell you one thing we'd do. We'd obey the next few verses in Ephesians 4 where Paul said:

> I therefore, the prisoner for the Lord, appeal to and beg you to walk (lead a life) worthy of the [divine] calling to which you have been called [with behavior that is a credit to the

summons to God's service, living as becomes you] with complete lowliness of mind (humility) and meekness (unselfishness, gentleness, mildness), with patience, bearing with one another and making allowances because you love one another. Be eager and strive earnestly to guard and keep the harmony and oneness of [and produced by] the Spirit in the binding power of peace (verses 1-3, AMPC).

Would you like to see another good picture of what walking in love looks like? This is it right here: Love makes allowances for other people. It doesn't cut them off just because they made a mistake or because they did something wrong. Love sticks with people even when they've messed up. It keeps loving others, regardless of whether it gets a loving response. Love *loves*—all the time, in every situation. It's not contentious or argumentative. It loves people no matter what they believe, think or say. *Love listens*

When we're walking in love, we don't shun other believers just because they don't agree with us on every point of doctrine. The love of God is the cure for division. We don't separate ourselves from them just because they emphasize one thing in the Bible and our church emphasizes another.

The love of God causes us to find common ground in Christ and set aside our differences.

Ken and I do this in our marriage. We look for common ground when there's something we don't agree on. If one of us wants to do one thing and the other wants to do something else, we don't let that disagreement divide us. We find a way to work things out and stay in harmony.

That's the way the Church should be. When we find ourselves in a doctrinal conflict, we should say to each other, "So what if you don't agree with me on some things? We don't have to see eye to eye on every detail. Let's center up on things we do agree on. Let's focus on the new birth and the fact that Jesus is Lord. Let's love one another like He said we should!"

If we'll take that approach, we can continue to grow in our love walk. We can build up the Body of Christ, as Ephesians 4:13 says:

> [That it might develop] until we all attain oneness in the faith and in the comprehension of the [full and accurate] knowledge of the Son of God, that [we might arrive] at really mature manhood (the completeness of personality which is nothing less than the standard height of Christ's own perfection), the measure of the stature of the fullness of the Christ and the completeness found in Him (AMPC).

The force of love is so powerful, it has a zero failure rate. It never, ever fails!

Speak Your Faith

For this cause, I bow my knees to You, Lord, the Father of our Lord Jesus Christ, of whom the whole family in heaven and earth is named, that You would grant to me, according to the riches of Your glory, to be strengthened with might by Your Spirit in my inner man. I believe that Christ dwells in my heart by faith, and that I, being rooted and grounded in love, am able to comprehend with all saints what is the breadth, and length, and depth, and height, and to know the love of Christ, which passes knowledge, that I might be filled with all the fullness of God. I believe I receive it now. In Jesus' Name. Amen!

Chapter 5

ENVY: AN ENEMY OF LOVE

A sound heart is the life of the flesh: but
envy the rottenness of the bones.

PROVERBS 14:30

The devil is a thief. He comes "to steal, and to kill, and to destroy" (John 10:10). So, it should come as no surprise to you that the moment you start bearing the fruit of love, he'll immediately set about to steal it. He'll try to introduce into your life things that are specifically designed to oppose and hinder your love walk. I call these things "enemies of love."

Just as the force of love produces victory and blessing in our lives, love's enemies open the door to Satan. They make us vulnerable to him so that he can get in and do his dirty work. If we know how to identify his strategies, however, we can guard ourselves against them. So, it's important for us to know what they are.

One enemy of love that's especially dangerous is the devilish force of *envy*.

Envy is a feeling of discontent and ill will because of another's advantages, possessions or success. It's a longing to possess something awarded to or achieved by another. It's closely associated with jealousy, which denotes a feeling of resentment that another has gained something one feels he or she more rightfully deserves.

First Corinthians 13:4 (AMPC) says emphatically, "Love is *never* envious"!

Love rejoices over other people's success. It celebrates when it sees them prosper. Envy does the opposite. It causes you to be sad when someone else gets ahead of you in some way. It causes you to think things like, *Look at that guy's new car! He doesn't work nearly as hard as I do! I'm the one who should be driving a new car!* Or, *Look at that woman's new house! She doesn't need a house that big and expensive. My family is much bigger than hers, and we're living in a house that's half that size.*

Even if we're walking in love, there are times when such thoughts come to all of us. They jump into our minds sometimes before we realize what's happening. But we don't have to entertain them. When a thought or feeling of envy comes, we can deal with it immediately and say, "No, that thought is not of God and I'm not taking it into my life. I rebuke you, envy. You're not love. You leave me. I'll not have that thought."

My father in the faith, Kenneth E. Hagin, used to say, "You can't stop the birds from flying over your head, but you can keep them from making a nest in your hair." And that's how it is with your thought life. You can't stop thoughts from coming, but you can refuse to give place to them— and you should if they come to you from Satan!

He puts thoughts into your mind to tempt and solicit you to do evil. He presents his envious ways of thinking to you like a salesman, hoping that you'll buy them. If you reject what he's trying to sell you, however, he's out of business. He has to go looking for another customer if you refuse to accept his ugly thoughts and take God's thoughts instead.

How do you take God's thoughts?

By filling your mind with the Scriptures, which are His written Word.

> *The Scriptures contain God's thoughts, and they're more powerful than anything the devil could ever come up with.*

As you read the Scriptures and meditate on them, they'll come alive in you and drive out everything that's contrary to them. God's thoughts about love will send envy packing. They will help you recognize it for what it is so you can identify it, deal with it as sin, and put it away from you.

That's important to do because envy will not only corrupt your love walk, it will neutralize your faith and put you at a great disadvantage. It will literally do damage to your life. It can even lead to sickness and disease and cause your physical body to deteriorate. As Proverbs 14:30 says, "A sound heart is the life of the flesh: but envy the rottenness of the bones."

I don't know about you, but I am not interested at all in having rotten bones! I want to depart from the evil of envy, so I can enjoy health in my body and *strength* in my bones (Proverbs 3:7-8, NKJV).

"Well," someone might say, "I think everyone has a little envy in them. I don't think it really qualifies as evil."

Then you'd better think again because the Bible puts it with the worst of the worst. It identifies envy as a work of the flesh and lists it in Galatians 5 alongside things like adultery, fornication, uncleanness, lasciousness, idolatry, witchcraft, hatred, variance, emulations, wrath, strife, seditions, heresies, murders, drunkenness and revellings (verses 19-21).

Envy is even referred to in Scripture as a symptom of a reprobate mind. It's named as a characteristic of people who, as Romans 1 says, are "being filled with all unrighteousness, sexual immorality, wickedness, covetousness, maliciousness; [are] full of envy...haters of God, violent, proud, boasters, inventors of evil things, disobedient to parents, undiscerning, untrustworthy, unloving, unforgiving, [and] unmerciful" (verses 29-31, NKJV).

Envy keeps really bad company! It isn't anything to mess around with. It's an ungodly, destructive force. It's a manifestation of darkness and an absolute enemy of love. As the Bible says:

> Love worketh no ill to his neighbor.... let us therefore cast off the works of darkness, and let us put on the armour of light. Let us walk honestly, as in the day; not in rioting and drunkenness, not in chambering and wantonness, not in strife and envying. But put ye on the Lord Jesus Christ, and make not provision for the flesh, to fulfil the lusts thereof (Romans 13:10-14).

> Let us not be desirous of vain glory, provoking one another, envying one another (Galatians 5:26).

> Wherefore laying aside all malice, and all guile, and hypocrisies, and envies, and all evil speakings, as newborn babes, desire the sincere milk of the word, that ye may grow thereby (1 Peter 2:1-2).

> But if ye have bitter envying and strife in your hearts, glory not, and lie not against the truth. This wisdom descendeth not from above, but is earthly, sensual, devilish. For where envying and strife is, there is confusion and every evil work (James 3:14-16).

Those last few verses are particularly sobering. They so clearly reveal the danger associated with envy, you ought to underline them in your Bible and put a little star by them. You ought to read them often so they become established in your heart. Then, whenever you're hit with a pang of envy:

Speak Your Faith

I refuse to receive envy! I refuse to allow confusion and every evil work to wreak havoc in my life. I choose instead to live and operate in the heavenly wisdom that comes from God. I rejoice when others do well because I delight in the Lord, and He gives me the desires of my heart. I know my God takes care of me and meets all my needs, and more—abundantly!

Running Over With Love, Joy and Contentment

If you'll live by His wisdom, you won't be very susceptible to envy. You won't have to be jealous of other people, because your heavenly Father will bless you as much as anyone around. As you delight in Him, "He shall give you the desires of your heart" (Psalm 37:4, NKJV).

What's more, as you delight in Him, spending time in His Word and in prayer, you'll become divinely content. You won't be inclined to envy someone else's lifestyle or possessions because you'll be busy basking in the richness of life in Jesus. You'll be praising Him, enjoying the satisfaction only He can give, and saying, "In Your presence is fullness of joy; at Your right hand are pleasures forevermore" (Psalm 16:11, NKJV).

On the other hand, if you don't take time to delight in the Lord, if you spend all your time on natural things and set your affections on them, you won't have that inner sense of contentment. You'll grow cold toward God, your spirit man will take second place, and you'll start looking to the things of this world to give you joy, peace and delight. You'll start noticing others who have things you want and don't yet have, and you'll become vulnerable to envy.

That happens to so many believers. They fall into the envy trap simply because they aren't giving God enough of their attention. They're not availing themselves of His appointed method of living the Christian life, which is to stay full of the Spirit through union and communion with Him!

The literal Greek translation of Ephesians 5:18 says, "Be being continually filled with the Spirit." In other words, maintain a constant spiritual overflow. Spend time in God's presence so that His Spirit rises up in you. Then you'll just naturally take upon yourself His characteristics.

> *Live so vitally connected to God and His Spirit that you're always running over with His love, joy and contentment.*

That's what always happens when you spend time with someone who has a strong personality. You begin taking on their characteristics and adopting their mannerisms. Without even thinking about it, you start talking like them and acting like them because you've been around them so much.

Your relationship with God works the same way. He has a strong personality and, as you fellowship with Him, it rubs off on you. You begin to look at things like He does. You begin to think His thoughts and walk according to His higher ways—and His ways are *always* right. His ways are *always* ways of love.

Envy, on the other hand, is the way of the devil. It comes to rob you and bring you failure. It comes to push you further away from getting that new car or home, or whatever it is you need. It comes to bring division and problems into your family, your church and the Body of Christ as a whole.

Envy is a diabolical thing. It has been used by Satan throughout history to stir up persecution against God's people. Remember how, in the Old Testament, Joseph's brothers sold him as a slave to the Egyptians and then told his father he'd been killed? Acts 7:9 says they did that because they were "moved with envy."

In the New Testament, the Jewish leaders delivered Jesus over to the Romans to be crucified. According to Mark 15:10, they did it "because of envy" (NKJV).

Remember all the trouble the Apostle Paul had to go through in the book of Acts just to preach the gospel? Almost all of it was caused by a spirit of envy. That spirit got on the unbelieving religious leaders of that day and drove them, in one situation after another, to try to destroy the Apostle Paul's ministry any way they could.

Envious Thorns in the Flesh

When Paul went to preach in Antioch in Pisidia, for example, he started out having a great series of meetings there. The people were so spiritually hungry "almost the whole city came together to hear the word of God. But when the Jews saw the multitudes, they were filled with envy; and contradicting and blaspheming, they opposed the things spoken by Paul" (Acts 13:44-45, NKJV). There was so much persecution stirred up against him, he eventually got thrown out of the city.

The same thing happened again in the city of Iconium. The enviers followed Paul there and stirred up the Gentiles against him. For a while, he kept preaching anyway. But as God continued to work signs and wonders to confirm the gospel, the enviers grew even more incensed. They poisoned people's minds against Paul and Barnabas until "the multitude of the city was divided" and "a violent attempt was made by both the Gentiles and Jews, with their rulers, to abuse and stone them" (Acts 14:4-5, NKJV).

After Paul and Barnabas fled for their lives from Iconium, they went to the city of Lystra—and the same envious people showed up! They "persuaded the people, and having stoned Paul, drew him out of the city, supposing he had been dead" (verse 19).

Just think about how overcome by envy those people were! They not only followed Paul from city to city harassing him, they actually tried to kill him. They thought they'd succeeded, too. They left Paul for dead, but "when the disciples gathered around him, he rose up and went into the city. And the next day he departed with Barnabas to Derbe" (verse 20, NKJV).

No matter what the spirit of envy did, it never did manage to overcome Paul! He always went right on traveling and preaching. His envious persecutors stuck with him like a "thorn in the flesh, the messenger of Satan to buffet" (2 Corinthians 12:7). But by God's grace, Paul always triumphed.

A little later in his ministry, after recovering again from being stoned, Paul went to Thessalonica, where there was a Jewish synagogue. Just as he always did, Paul preached the good news to them:

> And some of them believed, and consorted with Paul and Silas; and of the devout Greeks a great multitude, and of the chief women not a few. But the Jews which believed not, moved with envy, took unto them certain lewd fellows of the baser sort, and gathered a company, and set all the city on an uproar... (Acts 17:4-5).

Those in Thessalonica weren't the same ones who'd come against Paul in the other cities. They were a different group of people. But the spirit of envy on them acted the same way it always did. It drove the religious leaders to try to stop Paul from ministering.

Why did they want to stop him? They were envious of his success. Their influence was slipping away because he was getting results they weren't getting. He was operating in the power of God and winning people to Jesus.

We All Have to Watch Out for It

The same kind of envy that got hold of the religious people in Paul's day still rears its ugly head in the Church today. It shows up sometimes in relationships between believers, and it brings division into churches. It can even get hold of ministers.

The pastor of a small church, for example, can be tempted to envy the new church that opened up down the street—especially if that church attracted thousands of members seemingly overnight. He can find himself giving way to feelings of ill will and thoughts of discontent every time he drives by and sees it prospering. After a while, if he doesn't realize what's happening and repent, he'll find reasons to criticize what the pastor there is doing. He'll be telling everyone down at the coffee shop about all the flaws he sees in that pastor.

That's not love! Love is happy for them, and happy for Jesus because His kingdom is advancing, and He's being glorified.

Love rejoices when someone else is doing better than we are.

When we get aggravated by how well someone else or another minister is doing, that's the spirit of envy working in us, and it will keep us from prospering. It will interfere with our relationship with God and keep His power from moving in our own lives and churches. It will bring confusion into our ministries and open the door to every evil work of the devil.

"Well," you might say, "I'm not in the fivefold ministry. I'm just a member of a church."

That doesn't mean you don't have to watch out for envy. It finds ways to cause trouble in the Body of Christ through church members, too. You might be in church one Sunday morning and start feeling annoyed over something trivial—like how another believer looks. You might feel a little jealous because you think they're prettier or more handsome than you are. As the Sundays pass by, you might find yourself getting cranky when you see that person wearing a new outfit and getting a lot of compliments.

What should you do if that happens?

Identify the problem as envy, and refuse to give it any place in your heart. Instead of bringing division into the church by avoiding that person, go out of your way to express love toward him or her. Smile and say, "You certainly do look lovely today!" Then go on your way, asking God to bless that person and thanking Him for making him or her so pleasant to look at.

For those in the church who don't care about things like other people's appearance, envy may try to get them upset over a certain minister, for instance, who's teaching something they don't agree with and is drawing a big following. That's the trick the devil used on the New Testament church of Corinth. He injected envy into that congregation by getting them to fuss with each other about who their favorite preacher was.

"I think Apollos is the best," said one group.

"No, Paul came first," said another group. "We ought to follow him."

"You're all wrong!" someone else argued. "You ought to be like me and just follow after Jesus!"

The Corinthians apparently thought that argument was worth having. They thought it was very spiritual. But the Apostle Paul reprimanded them for it. He wrote to them and said, "I, brethren, could not speak unto you as unto spiritual, but as unto carnal, even as unto babes in Christ.... For ye are yet carnal: for whereas there is among you envying, and strife, and divisions, are ye not carnal, and walk as [unchanged] men?" (1 Corinthians 3:1, 3).

It doesn't matter how spiritually mature you might think you are, if you're saying things that bring division into the Body of Christ, you're being carnal! You're operating in the flesh and not in the spirit. When you're walking in the spirit, even if another believer gets into strife with you, do everything you can to maintain peace. Don't get into strife with that person. Don't cause more trouble in the church by going around saying the same ugly things about them they're saying about you (Proverbs 24:29). No, keep treating that person kindly because you're operating in love.

I'm not saying, of course, that if you stay free of envy, you'll be able to closely follow any preacher, regardless of what they teach. You need to be discerning. Although you can learn something from everyone who knows the Bible and loves the Lord, you need to stay away from unscriptural teachings that will damage your faith.

That's what I do. While I enjoy reading a variety of Christian authors and leaders, I avoid books written by people who don't tell me the truth. I don't listen to ministers who preach religious tradition and say things like God makes people sick or keeps them poor to teach them something.

I can't afford to listen to things like that! When sickness tries to come on me, I don't want to have to wonder, *Is this sickness from God?* I want to be confident that God wants me well and that by Jesus' stripes I was healed (1 Peter 2:24).

I feed my spirit only on teaching that reinforces the truth.

At the same time, though, I don't go around arguing with Christians who don't agree with me about everything. I don't go around putting up walls of division between me and them just because they don't believe exactly like I do. I endeavor to walk in love toward everyone. And I've found I can fellowship with almost any believer, as long as I remember I don't always have to express my opinions to them.

One time the Lord told Ken that the greatest problem He had with the Body of Christ was our "dogged determination to correct one another." I don't want Him to have that problem with me! I don't want to be always correcting other believers. That's not my responsibility, and it's not yours, either.

Our Christian brothers and sisters aren't our servants. They're servants of Jesus, and He's the only One who has the right to judge and correct them. He may lead us sometimes to go minister to another believer if they're getting pulled off into darkness. He may direct us to reach out to them and share the truth. But when He does, we're to approach that person in gentleness and meekness. We're not to go with the attitude, *I'm so brilliant and you're not, so I've come to talk to you.* No, we're to go clothed with the attitude of love.

As Cruel as the Grave

"But Gloria," you might say, "what about when I'm doing my best to walk in love, and someone just keeps on being mean to me?"

Follow the example of the Apostle Paul. He never let another person's bad treatment of him drive him off his God-ordained course. He kept ministering to people, even when they harassed him and caused him trouble. He kept choosing to walk in love and to pay "no attention to a suffered wrong" (1 Corinthians 13:5, AMPC).

If Paul could do that in his situation, certainly we can do it today. The worst most of us have to put up with is someone talking ugly about us. Paul suffered both verbal and physical abuse! He was blasphemed and publicly reviled. He was beaten, stoned and sent to prison where he was locked up for long periods of time.

Paul didn't deserve that kind of treatment! He wasn't doing anything wrong. He was just trying to help people by telling them about the love of Jesus. He was teaching the Word of God and getting people healed. Yet, he wound up being treated like a criminal for it.

Paul could have gotten mad about it had he yielded to his flesh. He could have become bitter toward his persecutors while sitting there in prison and spent his time and energy railing against them. But, thank God, he didn't do that! Had he yielded to his flesh, he wouldn't have written three-quarters of the New Testament, and we would be missing some of our most precious epistles because Paul wrote them while he was in prison.

We think prison is bad today, but it was far worse in Paul's day! His circumstances were more miserable than we can imagine. Yet, he continued to walk in the spirit. He spent time communicating with the Lord and stayed in love. Though he was in prison on many occasions, he made it his mission to be a blessing to the Church. He fulfilled that mission so well that he's still blessing us today, even though he's been in heaven for almost 2,000 years.

Envy may have put Paul in prison, but it couldn't get prison into him! He finished his life in victory. He lived to be an old man, and when he decided he was ready, he laid down his life for Jesus and went home to be with the Lord, saying:

> I have fought a good fight, I have finished my course, I have kept the faith: Henceforth there is laid up for me a crown of righteousness, which the Lord, the righteous judge, shall give me at that day (2 Timothy 4:7-8).

Paul is an inspiring example! Regardless of what he went through, he continued to yield to the force of love, and it kept him strong.

The strongest people in the world are those who walk in the love of God. When you operate in His love, He takes your part. He protects you. He keeps you and causes you to finish your course in triumph.

Satan can't do those things for you. He can't even bless the people who obey him. Everything he does turns into a curse. You can forget the stories you've heard about people who made deals with the devil, and because they did what he said, he made them happy, successful or rich. Those stories are lies. It's a ridiculous concept. There's no good in Satan, so no deal anyone makes with him will *ever* do that person any good.

Think about that the next time he tries to sell you on envy. Remember Song of Solomon 8:6 says, "Jealousy is cruel as the grave." Say no to that deadly thing. Treat it like the enemy that it is, and run it off with what God's Word says about love.

If you do fall prey to envy sometimes and stumble in your love walk, don't be discouraged. Just repent and let the Lord help you get back on track. He said in the Bible that all of us, as believers, are "taught of God to love one another" (1 Thessalonians 4:9). So look to Him to teach you. Let Him show you how to stay free of envy and make walking in love your supernaturally natural way of life!

Speak Your Faith

I refuse to walk in envy and jealousy. They are fruit of the flesh. I choose to walk in the love of God. I am born of Love. Love dwells in me. I rejoice when others are doing better than I am or when they get something I wanted. Because I walk in love, God takes my part. He keeps me and causes me to finish my course in triumph!

74

Chapter 6

STAY STRIFE FREE!

For where envying and strife is, there is
confusion and every evil work.

JAMES 3:16

Another enemy of love you want to watch out for is the enemy the
Bible calls *strife*. It's defined as "vigorous or bitter conflict, discord or
antagonism." It means "to quarrel, struggle or clash, to be in competition
or conflict."

Listed in the Scripture right alongside envy, strife is really Satan's top
weapon. It's the tool he uses to separate believers from one another. Since
he doesn't have the power to steal God's love out of our hearts, he uses
strife to make that love ineffective, so we won't be able to walk in its never-
failing power.

You've heard the phrase *divide and conquer?* That's the primary strat-
egy the devil uses against the Church. He tries to undermine it by getting
Christians to fuss and fight with each other. He does everything he can
to keep us apart because he's terrified we're all going to "come in the unity
of the faith, and of the knowledge of the Son of God, unto a perfect man,
unto the measure of the stature of the fulness of Christ" (Ephesians 4:13).

The day the Church comes into full unity will be the second-worst day of the devil's existence! (His worst day was the day Jesus defeated him in hell and rose from the dead.) Satan absolutely dreads that day because when we all come together in harmony with one another, he's totally helpless against us.

He can't do anything to stop the advancement of God's kingdom when the Church is operating as a united force. One day, before Jesus returns, we're going to do that. We're going to get so tuned in to the Holy Spirit that we'll all start walking in one accord. When that happens, even denominational differences won't divide us anymore. We'll all be listening to the Lord and following His directions. We'll be in agreement to a degree that hasn't been seen on earth since the days of the early Church.

Acts 2 says that in those days, believers came together with such "singleness of heart" they were absolutely unstoppable. Their numbers grew by leaps and bounds. The gospel spread like wildfire, "And the Lord added to the church daily those who were being saved" (verses 46-47, NKJV).

The devil remembers what that was like! It was terrible for him, and he doesn't want to go through it again. So he constantly tries to get us in disagreement with one another. He knows if he can succeed in doing that, we won't be any threat to him. He'll be able to run right over us because when we're in strife, we're on his territory. We're operating in his lowly, hellish kind of wisdom.

James 3:15-18 says:

> This wisdom descendeth not from above, but is earthly, sensual, devilish. For where envying and strife is, there is confusion and every evil work. But the wisdom that is from above is first pure, then peaceable, gentle, and easy to be intreated, full of mercy and good fruits, without partiality, and without hypocrisy. And the fruit of righteousness is sown in peace of them that make peace.

"But Gloria," someone might say, "I don't really think all strife is devilish. I don't think it's always such a hellish force."

Well, God says it is, and He's always right! Whatever He tells us in the Bible is how things are and, according to these verses, you can't live in strife and enjoy a good, peaceful life at the same time. It's impossible.

> *God's wisdom opens the door for you to walk in His blessings.*

The devil's wisdom and God's wisdom are contrary to one another. The devil's wisdom robs you of God's blessings. It opens the door for Satan to come into your life and bring confusion and every evil work.

Strife Will Keep You Carnal

If the devil can keep you in strife, he can wipe out all the good things that belong to you as a Christian. You may still go to heaven when you die, but you won't have any fun getting there, because strife will keep you walking after the flesh instead of the spirit. It will cause you to remain carnal instead of spiritual.

As we've already seen, that's what happened to the Christians in Corinth. They got into envy and strife and got stuck being carnally minded. As a result, they stopped growing in the Lord. Their spiritual capacity became so limited that the Apostle Paul had to write them and say:

> I brethren, could not speak unto you as unto spiritual, but as unto carnal, even as unto babes in Christ. I have fed you with milk, and not with meat: for hitherto ye were not able to bear it, neither yet now are ye able. For ye are yet carnal: for whereas there is among you envying, and strife, and divisions, are ye not carnal, and walk as men? (1 Corinthians 3:1-3)

Think about what a sad situation that was! Those people had the great Apostle Paul right there wanting to impart revelation to them. They had one of the most powerful preachers of all time wanting to feed them the meat of the Word. But they couldn't receive it. They were so busy bickering with one another, all they could handle was a little milk.

It takes the meat of the Word to grow spiritually strong and be blessed. So by continuing to fuss with one another, the Corinthians closed the door to their own spiritual growth. They locked themselves into remaining immature and carnal.

Carnal Christians are a miserable species of being! They're born again, and they know enough about God to keep them from enjoying sin. But they don't know enough to live free of it. They end up in trouble, time and again, because they keep reacting to things in the flesh.

If someone wrongs them, instead of taking no account of it and walking in love, they get all riled up. They take up for themselves and fight for their own rights. That's always what the flesh does. When it's not under the spirit's dominion, it behaves selfishly and seeks its own. In the process, it steals your peace, hinders your progress and keeps you from prospering in God.

I'll never forget when Ken and I first realized this. We were just beginning to learn how to live by faith in God's Word. We were desperate for a manifestation of His prosperity in our lives. We'd already tried to prosper on our own and failed miserably. So, we were searching the Scriptures to find out how to do things God's way.

When we saw what He said about strife in James 3, we both knew right away that if we wanted to live in THE BLESSING of God, we'd have to get along with each other. So that's what we decided to do. We committed to live in harmony and agreement and to stay out of strife.

From that day to this, we've kept that commitment. Although we've had to work at it, we've learned to be quick to resolve whatever disagreements crop up between us. We've learned that it's more important to avoid strife in our home than to appear justified. It's more important to maintain the harmony between us than to win an argument, get our own way or prove we're right. If we slip and say something unloving to each other, we repent right away and forgive one another. We keep the door closed to strife in our home. This keeps the door open for us to live in divine prosperity and peace.

Of course, we've also been diligent to keep strife out of our relationships with other people, but we've remained most watchful at home because many years ago, the Lord said to me:

If you allow Satan to stop you with strife at your front door, you'll be no threat to him anywhere else.

As most everyone knows, the easiest place in the world to give in to selfishness is at home. Unlike out in public where people will judge us or even reject us if we act too ugly, at home there aren't many natural barriers to restrain us. We aren't concerned about what other people think of us there. We're not trying to be nice to maintain our reputation. We know our family has to put up with us, so we tend to feel a little freer to give in to our flesh and act as though what we do at home doesn't really count.

In reality, however, what we do at home counts a great deal! The people there are the nearest and dearest to us. Our relationships with them make all the difference. If you're married, when you and your spouse are at odds with one another, your whole life is negatively affected. Even though things at work may be going well, you'll be miserable if strife is bringing hell into your relationship with your husband or wife.

If your marriage is harmonious, on the other hand, your life can be heavenly. You can be happy even though in other areas you may be dealing with negative circumstances. Better yet, when you and your spouse are in harmony, you can do something together that will change negative circumstances. You can act on Matthew 18:19 that says, "If two of you shall agree on earth as touching any thing that they shall ask, it shall be done for them of my Father which is in heaven."

That's a powerful way to pray! But you can't successfully pray that way if, right after you say, "Amen," you go right back to living in strife. For your prayers to be effective, you must cultivate a lifestyle of love and agreement. You must make it your habit to be sweet and lovely to one another. You must make living in harmony and walking together in love the goal of your marriage.

If you'll do that, not only will your prayers be answered, you'll never be bothered with divorce. The subject won't even come up. When husbands and wives are both loving each other with the love of God, they don't want to leave each other; they want to be together! They want to keep enjoying one another's company.

Keeping strife out of your home will also benefit your children because, for better or for worse, you're always setting patterns for them. They naturally tend to reproduce what they see in you so, when they grow up, their home will probably be much like yours.

Even children who don't like the way things are in the home where they're raised, usually wind up following their parents' example. Children who grow up with alcoholic parents, for instance, are likely to have problems with alcohol themselves. Children who grow up with abuse, even though they hate being subjected to it themselves, will often perpetuate that abuse with their own children.

Whether you live for God or you live for the devil, you're leaving an inheritance for your children and grandchildren. So, give them a heritage of love, and peace and well-being. Teach them to treat strife as an enemy, and to live in harmony and love at home.

Don't Damage Your Spiritual Reputation

Another very important place strife must be treated as an enemy is in the local church. If Satan manages to stir up strife there, he can rob a whole body of believers of their effectiveness and influence for God on the earth. He can use their conflicts with one another to give Christianity a bad name.

We're to be known in the world for the way we love each other (John 13:35). So when strife erupts among us, it damages our spiritual reputation. It becomes a tool the devil can use to convince people that Christianity is just another religion without any real life or power in it.

Strife is a powerful weapon of Satan! It can stop the Body of Christ because everything we do for God must be done by faith. Since faith works by love, believers can't be in strife and faith at the same time. Therefore, strife can actually paralyze revival in the earth. It can keep individual believers from growing spiritually and being witnesses for Jesus. It can thwart the advancement of the kingdom of God.

> For the whole Law [concerning human relationships] is complied with in the one precept, You shall love your neighbor as [you do] yourself. But if you bite and devour one another [in partisan strife], be careful that you [and your whole fellowship] are not consumed by one another (Galatians 5:14-15, AMPC).

Talk about a dangerous foe! Strife is an enemy that can cause a whole church to be consumed. It can put entire congregations under Satan's thumb. It can cause us to stop walking in the spirit and step over into the realm of the flesh.

The moment believers yield to strife, we give the devil mastery over us.

When we're walking in the flesh, we're not going to be any threat to the devil. We're not going to be pulling down his strongholds and causing him to flee. We're not going to be having powerful prayer meetings and seeing great results.

However, if we get into harmony and agreement, we will be doing those things. We'll be defeating the devil at every turn because agreement will get us out of the flesh and back in the spirit. It will allow our faith to work so that whatever we ask in prayer will be done for us (Matthew 21:22).

Agreement is God's answer to strife! It turns the tables on the devil and enables us to "overcome evil with good" (Romans 12:21). It causes God's presence to manifest in our midst. The more we promote an atmosphere of harmony in the Church, the more of His power He'll pour out through us because He'll be able to trust us to not hurt anyone.

This is why Ken and I are so watchful to keep strife out of our ministry. We've seen what can happen when someone comes in with a strife-prone personality. That person can cause conflict to erupt wherever he or she goes. On occasion, we've had some people here who did that, and we didn't keep them around very long. Even though we loved them, we followed the instructions in Romans 16:17 which says, "Mark them which cause divisions and offences...and avoid them."

We can't afford to have dividers on our staff! For THE BLESSING of God to operate in this ministry in full measure, we have to be in harmony with one another. If there's conflict among us, the anointing won't flow like it should.

Don't expect God to manifest His glory in a strife-filled atmosphere. He absolutely detests it. As Proverbs 6:16-19 says:

> These six things doth the Lord hate: yea, seven are an abomination unto him: a proud look, a lying tongue, and hands that shed innocent blood, an heart that deviseth wicked imaginations,

feet that be swift in running to mischief, a false witness that speaketh lies, and he that soweth discord among brethren.

Notice that, according to those verses, strife, like envy, runs with very bad company! It hangs around with things like lying and murder. Gossiping, backbiting, spreading rumors about some bad thing someone did or said is all part of strife. In the sight of God, strife is a very serious offense, and many believers yield to it.

Some do it almost professionally, seemingly on purpose. Others do it without being aware of it. They might see another believer stumble or sin and just assume it's their duty to go and tell everyone about it. It's never a believer's duty to gossip about someone. It's our duty to walk in love, and that's not how love acts!

Love doesn't expose other people's mistakes. It doesn't provoke people in church to point fingers at a believer who's done wrong and perpetuate his or her problem by passing it around. As Proverbs 10:12 says, "Hatred stirreth up strifes: but love covereth all sins."

Love believes the best of every person. Love prays for the person who's fallen into sin and believes God for him or her. Love tries to shield and restore the person. It causes us to do for a fallen brother or sister what we would want them to do for us if we were in their shoes.

Yes, Even if It's the Pastor

"But what if the person who's doing something wrong is very important?" someone might say. "What if it's the pastor?"

That's still no excuse to stir up strife in church. The pastor is not your servant. He's God's servant, and God can take care of him. You're not responsible to be his judge or to go around warning everyone about what you've heard he may have done.

Most likely, you don't know all the facts, anyway. Generally, in those situations, we don't. We're just putting together rumors and hearsay without fully understanding the whole story.

That's why, when we hear something unsettling about a minister, it's best just to do what the Bible tells us to do. It says, "Judge nothing before the time, until the Lord come, who both will bring to light the hidden things of darkness, and will make manifest the counsels of the hearts" (1 Corinthians 4:5).

In other words, no matter what happens, don't judge your pastor. If he isn't behaving as he should, and you don't feel you can follow him anymore, then leave and find another church where things are right. But don't sow discord as you're leaving. Just quietly withdraw. Then go wherever the Lord leads you, and continue to do everything you can to keep from stirring up strife.

Avoiding strife is always the wisest thing to do in any situation! The Bible confirms it time and again. The Scriptures say:

> A wrathful man stirreth up strife: but he that is slow to anger appeaseth strife (Proverbs 15:18).

> A froward man soweth strife: and a whisperer separateth chief friends (Proverbs 16:28).

> He that is slow to anger is better than the mighty; and he that ruleth his spirit than he that taketh a city (verse 32).

> Better is a dry morsel, and quietness therewith, than an house full of sacrifices with strife (Proverbs 17:1).

> The beginning of strife is as when water first trickles [from a crack in a dam]; therefore stop contention before it becomes worse and quarreling breaks out (verse 14, AMPC).

He loveth transgression that loveth strife: and he that exalteth his gate seeketh destruction (verse 19).

It is an honour for a man to cease from strife: but every fool will be meddling (Proverbs 20:3).

And the servant of the Lord must not strive; but be gentle unto all men, apt to teach, patient (2 Timothy 2:24).

Do nothing from factional motives [through contentiousness, strife, selfishness, or for unworthy ends] or prompted by conceit and empty arrogance. Instead, in the true spirit of humility (lowliness of mind) let each regard the others as better than and superior to himself [thinking more highly of one another than you do of yourselves] (Philippians 2:3, AMPC).

"But Gloria," someone might say. "I have to deal with people in my life who have really mistreated me. It's hard for me to avoid getting into strife with them."

I understand. But strife won't help you deal with those people. Walking in the love of God will. When you respond to them in love and refuse to become angry and contentious, you stay in command of your interactions with them. You're able to maintain your temper and keep things from getting out of hand.

Love keeps you in the light.

The enemies of love drag you into darkness. They open the door to Satan and give him a place in your life. He can only operate in darkness. He can't operate in the light, so when he tempts you to get into strife, say no to him. Slam the door in his face, keep walking in love and stay in the light.

That's the only safe place to be!

Speak Your Faith

I walk in the love of God. I respond in love, and I refuse to become angry and contentious. I refuse to enter into strife. I stay in the light as He is in the light. I am patient and kind, and I maintain my temper. I keep it back and still it. I open my mouth with wisdom, and in my tongue is the law of kindness!

Chapter 7

DON'T GET TOO BIG FOR YOUR BRITCHES

> *Love is patient and kind. Love is not
> jealous or boastful or proud.*
> 1 CORINTHIANS 13:4, NLT

Another enemy of love mentioned in 1 Corinthians 13 is so dangerous, we're warned about its perils all through the Bible. It's something we want to be quick to spot and stop the minute it tries to get a hold on us.

It's the enemy of pride.

Pride is defined as "a high or inordinate opinion of one's own dignity, importance, merit or superiority." It's an overinflated or exaggerated sense of one's self. It's associated with haughtiness, arrogant behavior and conceit. It's what we used to refer to as "getting too big for your britches."

The opposite of love, pride is totally self-centered. Where love focuses on God and on being a blessing to others, pride causes a person to focus on self and other people's opinions of him or her. It makes the person so self-conscious, so concerned about image and reputation that, as Psalm 10:4 says, "In all his thoughts there is no room for God" (NIV).

Some people allow pride to hinder them from taking even the first step toward God. They'll go to church with a friend, hear the gospel preached, and want to make Jesus their Lord, but then refuse to respond to the invitation at the end of the service. They'll stay in their seats and keep silent rather than praying the prayer of salvation because they're afraid of what other people will think.

At times, pride even has that effect on believers. It gets us preoccupied with ourselves and keeps us from pressing further into God. Christians, for example, who haven't yet received the Baptism in the Holy Spirit, might hear a sermon about speaking in other tongues. But pride might stop them from believing and acting on it. They might say to themselves, *It would be wonderful to be able pray out of my spirit, to pray beyond what I know, and pray out the perfect will of God, but I'd look so foolish! What would my friends think if they heard me?*

Believers who have pressed past those concerns and gone on to receive the Baptism in the Holy Spirit might let pride hinder them in other ways. They might let it throw a stumbling block in their paths every time God tells them to do anything the least bit unusual. They might start thinking about themselves and their reputation and stop short of obeying God.

In my early years in ministry, although I was Spirit-filled, I was still fairly timid and quiet, so I was inclined to be reserved. But I had a strong desire to walk with God, so I began to pray, "Lord, show me how to follow Your Spirit. I just want to obey You. You tell me what to do, and I'll do it."

He answered, of course. But when He'd tell me to do something that was a little out of the ordinary, I'd be hesitant to step out on it. I was afraid I might look foolish. Fear isn't of God because He is Love, and "there is no fear in love" (1 John 4:18). So the problem was obvious: I was being held back by pride.

So what did I do about it?

I'm happy to say, I chose to resist pride and yield to love!

I chose to put my love for God first and to love His people enough to do whatever He told me, particularly when I began teaching Healing School in our Believers' Conventions. I decided, *I am going to obey the Holy Spirit. Whatever He leads me to do, I'll do it—even if, in the eyes of others, it makes me look silly.*

"But Gloria," you might ask, "weren't you concerned about losing your dignity?"

I was at first, but then I looked up *dignity* in the dictionary and found out that one of its meanings is "to be self-possessed." I don't want to be self-possessed. I want to be God-possessed! I want His Spirit to have His way in my life.

God's people believe and obey Him, even when He tells them to do things that don't always look sensible or reasonable to anyone else.

That's what God's faith people did in the Bible. Look at Joshua, for instance. It didn't look reasonable for him to do what God said at the battle of Jericho. It didn't make sense for him to march the Israelites around the walls of the city for seven days without saying a word, and then tell them to shout on the last day for no apparent reason. Yet Joshua followed God's instructions and, as a result, the walls of Jericho fell down flat (Joshua 6:20)!

That story would have turned out differently, however, if Joshua had let pride get involved. Instead of obeying God, he could have come up with a more "sensible" battle plan. He could have done things his own way and closed the door on God's supernatural power. But the walls of Jericho wouldn't have fallen down.

Psalm 138:6 says, "Though the Lord be high, yet hath he respect unto the lowly: but the proud he knoweth afar off." Joshua couldn't afford for the Lord to be *afar off* when he was trying to conquer Jericho. And we can't either, when we're facing the challenges in our lives. If we want to walk in supernatural victory, we have to keep the door wide open to God by walking in love and remaining humble. We have to say no to the enemy of pride!

An Ugly, Evil Thing

As believers, we don't really have any reason to be proud, anyway. All the good things in us, as well as what we have, come from God (James 1:17). We didn't produce them ourselves through our own great ability. They're ours through Jesus and the grace that flows to us through Him. No matter how talented we may be in the natural, apart from Him, we wouldn't be able to do anything of real value. It's because He loves us and gives to us generously, out of His own abundance, that we're so richly blessed.

The more we mature in God, the clearer that becomes to us. The better we know Him, the more we steer away from pride because we realize how totally dependent we are on Him. Someone wrote to me one time, years ago, after hearing me preach on this and said, "In the natural, as you grow up, you become less dependent on your parents. But as you grow up in the spirit, you become more dependent on your Father."

That's absolutely true! It was even true for Jesus when He was on earth. He said, "Believest thou not that I am in the Father, and the Father in me? the words that I speak unto you I speak not of myself: but the Father that dwelleth in me, he doeth the works" (John 14:10).

As Jesus' disciples, we should have the same attitude. We should give all the praise and glory to God for the victories we win and the successes we enjoy. Instead of getting into pride we should worship and thank Him.

Speak Your Faith

Lord, thank You! You're the reason I'm blessed! You're the reason I'm born again and headed for heaven instead of lost in sin and headed for hell. You're the reason I have food on my table and clothes on my back. Where would I be without You, God? Without Your mercy and grace, I'd be an absolute zero. I wouldn't have anything at all! Thank You for loving me and blessing me!

God appreciates it when you take that attitude. He responds well to gratitude and thankfulness but not to pride. He considers it an ugly, evil thing. As the Bible says:

These...things doth the Lord hate: yea, seven are an abomination unto him: A proud look, a lying tongue, and hands that shed innocent blood (Proverbs 6:16-17).

The fear of the Lord is to hate evil: pride, and arrogancy, and the evil way, and the froward mouth, do I hate (Proverbs 8:13).

An high look, and a proud heart, and the plowing of the wicked, is sin (Proverbs 21:4).

Therefore pride compasseth [the wicked] about as a chain; violence covereth them as a garment (Psalm 73:6).

For all that is in the world, the lust of the flesh, and the lust of the eyes, and the pride of life, is not of the Father, but is of the world (1 John 2:16).

Notice in those verses, pride is tied up with things like lies, violence, wickedness and sin. It's referred to as one of the things God hates. Why does He hate it? Because He loves us and wants us to enjoy His best, and pride cuts us off from it. Pride hinders our connection with Him and stops us from receiving His blessings. It puts us over on the devil's turf and makes us vulnerable to his destructive works.

If we understood the kind of damage pride can do in our lives, we'd hate it as much as God does. We'd avoid it like a plague because we'd realize that:

> Pride goeth before destruction, and an haughty spirit before a fall (Proverbs 16:18).

> A man's pride shall bring him low: but honour shall uphold the humble in spirit (Proverbs 29:23).

> When pride cometh, then cometh shame: but with the lowly is wisdom (Proverbs 11:2).

> By pride comes nothing but strife, but with the well-advised is wisdom (Proverbs 13:10, NKJV).

> The pride of thine heart hath deceived thee (Obadiah 1:3).

Look again at that last verse. It says pride is a deceiver. It tricks people into thinking they're high and exalted and then deceives them into doing things that bring them down.

Pride will even try to deceive you into thinking you can get away with sin! It will tell you, "Hey, other people might not be able to handle a little flirting at work or watching a few ungodly movies, but that stuff won't hurt me. I can indulge in it for a little bit, and if it starts giving me trouble, I'll just repent."

I've even known of ministers who fell for that deception! They got prideful over the success they were having in God. They began to think, *I'm someone special. I don't have to obey the Word like everybody else does. I can do whatever I want, and God will still back me because I'm His man.* Before long, their ministries were ruined.

The same kind of thing can happen to believers who aren't in full-time ministry. A business executive, for instance, might become wealthy and so successful he gets the idea he can snort a little cocaine, and it won't cause any problems for him. Despite having seen other people get hooked on drugs he might think, *I'm too smart to let that happen to me. I've got it all together. I'm Mister Big.*

Another person might start drinking alcohol with the same attitude. They might be deceived by pride into thinking, *I'm too strong to ever succumb to this stuff. I have enough self-discipline to drink whenever I want and stop whenever I want. I'd never let my drinking get control of me.*

Watch Out for That Snake!

This is always how pride works. Like all temptations, it slips into your thoughts first. Then, once it gets a place there, it deceives you into doing sinful things that will defile you. As Jesus said:

> For from within, out of the heart of men, proceed evil thoughts, adulteries, fornications, murders, thefts, covetousness, wickedness, deceit, lasciviousness, an evil eye [envy], blasphemy, pride, foolishness: all these evil things come from within, and defile the man (Mark 7:21-23).

Pride is subtle. It won't come barging in, announcing itself and saying, "I'm pride, and I'm here to get you to sin!" It will just try to creep in undercover here and there. It will try to stay enshrouded in darkness so you won't notice it.

This is why we need to study what the Scriptures say about it. God's Word brings things into the light. It exposes pride for what it is and reveals its deceptive tactics.

As we've seen time and again, deception is the devil's game. Regardless of how spiritually mature we become, he never stops trying to deceive us.

> *The devil will always come and try to steal, kill and destroy, so we must perpetually shine the light of the Word on him.*

As 1 Peter 5:8 says, he is an adversary, and we must "be vigilant."

To be *vigilant* means "to stay awake, watch, or stay alert to avoid danger." It's doing what Ken and I do when we're walking around the creek at our prayer cabin. There are a lot of water moccasins and other snakes there, so we watch our step and tread cautiously. When we turn over our old fishing boat, after it's been sitting unused for a while, we're always careful to watch out for snakes!

That's the way we as believers need to be in our love walk. We want to be vigilant and on the alert against the enemies that come against it. We must be very watchful so that when the devil slithers up next to us and tempts us with pride, we can resist him with our words of faith.

Speak Your Faith

> *No, Devil! I rebuke you. I refuse to receive prideful thoughts. I'm going to walk in the spirit, and stay in love!*

Pride will always bring us low (Proverbs 29:23). It is the nature of the devil. Resisting it is crucial to our safety and success in life. If we don't do it, we put ourselves in a very dangerous position. James 4:6 says, "God resisteth the proud, but giveth grace unto the humble." Why is that? Because the devil is a creature of pride. That's what got him into trouble. You can't walk in the pride of life, being your own god, and walk in faith toward God at the same time because you must depend on God to walk in faith.

So don't allow yourself to get into that place! You won't make any progress in life. Basically, you've gone as far as you're going to go. On the other hand, when you're flowing in God's grace, no one can stop you from advancing. When you submit to Him and let go of the pride that's been pushing Him away, He'll personally see to it that you succeed:

> Humble yourselves therefore under the mighty hand of God, that he may exalt you in due time (1 Peter 5:6).

> Submit yourselves therefore to God. Resist the devil, and he will flee from you (James 4:7).

One way you humble yourself and submit to God is to simply believe what He says in His Word, the Bible. When you read the Scriptures or hear someone preach from the Word that "by [Jesus'] stripes ye were healed" (1 Peter 2:24), accept that it's the truth. When you find out the Bible says it's God's will for you to prosper (3 John 2), receive it as the truth. Why is that important? Because Jesus said in Matthew 9:29, "According to your faith be it unto you."

So don't treat God's Word with skepticism. Don't go away after hearing it preached and say, "That can't be right! My church teaches such and such. I see what the Bible says, but I'm going to stick with what I was taught growing up." No, that's pride—pride in your denomination or your religious heritage—and it will push God away from you. In other words, it will keep you from receiving His blessings in your life.

As believers, we're not called to sit in judgment on the Scriptures. We're not supposed to try to figure out if we agree with them or decide if acting on them will be to our advantage. We're just supposed to humble ourselves beneath God's mighty hand and do whatever He says. Why? Because God is smarter than we are! His ways are higher than our ways.

When we believe and obey His Word, it keeps us under His protective covering. It keeps the devil under our feet.

When we're living in obedience to God, it keeps the devil from getting a foothold in our lives. Sin opens the door to him. But when we're obedient to God and submitted to Him, the devil has to do what we say and flee when we resist him (James 4:7). So, if we'll just walk according to the Scriptures, he'll be defeated, and we'll always come out on top!

Don't Be a Know-It-All

One vital area where obeying the Scriptures will protect us from pride is in our relationships with other believers. It's easy for us to let arrogance slip in, particularly when we're fellowshipping with those who aren't as strong in the Lord as we are. We can be tempted to act like know-it-alls and correct people in ways that leave them feeling inferior or embarrassed.

The New Testament warns us against that. It says:

> Don't criticize and speak evil about each other, dear brothers (James 4:11, TLB).

> Accept the one whose faith is weak, without quarreling over disputable matters (Romans 14:1, NIV).

> Look after each other so that not one of you will fail to find God's best blessings. Watch out that no bitterness takes root among you, for as it springs up it causes deep trouble, hurting many in their spiritual lives.... Continue to love each other with true brotherly love. Don't forget to be kind (Hebrews 12:15, 13:1-2, TLB).

> Be humble and gentle. Be patient with each other, making allowance for each other's faults because of your love (Ephesians 4:2, TLB).

When we're walking in love, we won't criticize other Christians for their faults and failures. If they're not as knowledgeable of the Word as we are, we won't argue with them about the Bible and make them feel like they're not as spiritual as we are. We'll minister to them in a way that uplifts them.

If they don't have all the light we have, we'll meet them where they are. If they don't know anything about divine healing and don't believe it's for today, but they're born again, we'll fellowship with them about how wonderful it is to be saved and to know we're going to heaven. We'll let them know, above all, that they are loved by God and loved by us.

> *God's love through you will open the hearts of others to learn more about the Word from you.*

God's love in you will cause you to be kind to them and prevent you from saying things that would plant seeds of bitterness in them. It will keep you from rejecting them just because you think they're wrong about something or they've made a mistake.

Instead of saying, "OK, I'm done with this person because he or she didn't act right," love will make you take a humbler attitude. It will make you think, *Well, sometimes I'm wrong, too, and I don't want people to reject me. So I'm going to be tolerant in this situation. I'm going to make allowances for this brother's mistake.*

Have you ever noticed how we as parents tend to make allowances for the imperfections in our children? Someone else's child might do something wrong, and we'll get totally exasperated about it. But when our children do the same thing, our inclination is to overlook it. Instead of criticizing them, we're likely to say, "Well, they were just tired," or, "They're hungry. That's the reason they misbehaved."

Why do we respond differently to our own children? Because the love we have for them goes beyond their faults. It causes us to want to protect and defend them regardless of what they do.

That's the way it's supposed to be in the Church! *We're a spiritual family.* We're to love one another unconditionally. We're to support and pray for one another and overlook one another's faults because love is what makes this family work.

When love isn't manifesting among us, gaps open up between us and the devil gets in. We become critical toward one another and miss out on "God's best blessings" (Hebrews 12:15, TLB). We start fighting each other and tearing each other down so that in the end, none of us win.

When love *is* manifesting among us, we're undefeatable. We can overcome anything. Because we're lifting each other up instead of lifting ourselves up in pride, God's love causes us to triumph. Its power goes to work in us as individual believers and as a spiritual family and makes sure we don't fail!

Maintaining a Pride-Free Home

"But what about my natural family?" someone might ask. "How are things going to work there? I'm the only one in it who knows anything about God."

Well, love has to start somewhere! In your family, it can start with you. If you'll walk in unconditional love toward your unsaved family members, God will come right into the midst of them. If you'll treat them the way the Bible says and pray for God to send laborers across their paths to share the Word with them, you can win your whole family to the Lord.

I can testify to this personally. I'm the oldest of seven children, and when I was born again, no one in my family but me knew the Lord. Today, however, my entire family knows and loves Jesus! Why? Because

Ken and I took the Word of God, got it into our hearts, and set ourselves to love those family members. We opened our hearts to them, and they became interested in what we have.

When my whole family gets together now, we have a great time, both spiritually and naturally. We all love one another. We stick with one another through thick and thin.

If someone does something that's not right, we don't turn our backs on them. We don't say, "You hurt my feelings," and cut off contact with them. We keep standing by them and praying for them. We keep coming together and giving ourselves for one another until things get turned around.

The same thing can happen in your family. As you continue to love them and live by faith in the Word, they'll eventually notice. They'll see the testimony of your life and say, "What is it you have that makes you so pleasant and easy to get along with? What is it that gives you such peace, even when things around you are in turmoil?" Then, you can tell them about Jesus, and they can come to know Him, too!

There's nothing more wonderful than a pride-free, love-ruled family!

It makes life so sweet. That's one reason the Bible has so much to say about family relationships. It's why the New Testament says to those of us who are married, for instance, to stop fighting for the top spot in our marriages, put the other person first, and obey the instructions in Ephesians 5:

> Wives, submit yourselves unto your own husbands, as unto the Lord. For the husband is the head of the wife, even as Christ is the head of the church: and he is the saviour of the body. Therefore as the church is subject unto Christ, so let

the wives be to their own husbands in every thing. Husbands, love your wives, even as Christ also loved the church, and gave himself for it.... So ought men to love their wives as their own bodies. He that loveth his wife loveth himself. For no man ever yet hated his own flesh; but nourisheth and cherisheth it, even as the Lord the church: For we are members of his body, of his flesh, and of his bones.

For this cause shall a man leave his father and mother, and shall be joined unto his wife, and they two shall be one flesh. This is a great mystery: but I speak concerning Christ and the church. Nevertheless let every one of you in particular so love his wife even as himself; and the wife see that she reverence her husband (verses 22-25, 28-33).

Ladies, you've got to brace up for this. According to those verses, the way you love your husband is to show reverence for him. *Reverence* means "to notice, regard, honor, prefer, venerate, esteem, defer to, praise, love and admire exceedingly." When you treat your husband like that, he'll generally be easier to get along with. When you don't, he's likely to get cranky!

Men, the reverse is also true. If you treat your wife like her happiness and well-being is as important to you as your own, she'll just naturally want to bless you. It's easy for a wife to submit to a husband who loves her like Christ loves the Church.

It's also easier for your children to submit to you as their parents in that kind of atmosphere. So, set the example for them and teach them that the Bible says:

Children, obey your parents in the Lord: for this is right. Honour thy father and mother; which is the first command- ment with promise; that it may be well with thee, and thou mayest live long on the earth. And, ye fathers, provoke not your children to wrath: but bring them up in the nurture and admonition of the Lord (Ephesians 6:1-4).

Teach your children that you want them to obey you not because you're puffed up and want to be the boss of everything, but because you want things to go well with them like the Bible says. You want them to operate like God says and be blessed. Make a commitment before God that you'll not be harsh and overbearing toward them, but you'll treat them with kindness and compassion. When you do have to correct them strongly, be sure you do it in the love of God.

Children want to be loved, and Proverbs 22:6 says if you "train up a child in the way he should go...when he is old, he will not depart from it." So, if you make the love of God the law of your home and train your children in it, they won't be inclined to rebel or run away from you when they grow up. They'll want to stay close to you. And even if, like the prodigal son, they do try to go their own way for a while, they'll always come back home again—to faith, family and God!

Chapter 8

DRINK IN GOD'S BLESSINGS— WITH JOY!

Therefore with joy shall ye draw water
out of the wells of salvation.

ISAIAH 12:3

Now that we've established the foundation of love, we can go ahead and talk about the next fruit of the spirit listed in Galatians 5: the force of joy. According to the dictionary, *joy* is "a very glad feeling, happiness, great pleasure, or delight." Like love, it's something everyone wants, yet most are unable to find because the last place they'd ever think to look is in God.

Due to religious tradition and the lies of the devil, God isn't generally known for being joyful. He's usually thought to be (at best) very somber, and (at worst), downright grumpy or perhaps even angry. According to the Bible, however, joy is one of the primary hallmarks of His nature. He not only has joy in abundance, it flows out of Him to such a degree that

103

the psalmist David said to Him, "In thy presence is fulness of joy; [and] at thy right hand there are pleasures for evermore" (Psalm 16:11).

Many believers are going to be surprised when they get to heaven! It's not a long-faced, sad place. Everyone there is smiling and shouting for joy.

One person I read about who had a vision of heaven saw a choir there, standing on a platform in front a huge congregation. The people in the choir wore beautiful robes and, at first, they seemed very proper and quiet. They moved up to the front with dignity like you might expect at most churches. Then suddenly, they all started praising the Lord. They broke out of that dignified stance and began to dance and shout. The joy of the Lord took over the whole place, and it got loud!

Did you know there's a scripture in Isaiah that talks about a time when the praise got so loud in the throne room of God, it moved the doorposts (Isaiah 6:4)? That's the kind of thing that happens in heaven. Everyone is so alive, so turned on to the Lord and so full of joy, they just overflow with it!

Many times, believers who get a glimpse of heaven get so excited about it they actually lose their desire to stay here on earth. They see what life is like over on the other side and decide to go ahead and move there. I've heard people who died, went to heaven and had to come back, testify they would have stayed in heaven if they'd had their choice. Once they got into the Lord's presence and experienced the fullness of His joy, they didn't want to leave!

We don't have to wait to get to heaven to walk in the joy of the Lord. We can do it right here and now because we have Jesus living inside us, and Hebrews 1:9 says God has anointed Him with "the oil of gladness." Joy is already inside us.

Our Lord Jesus is a joyful Lord! He put His joy in us when we were born again. It's a powerful force, not like the fleeting and temporal happiness the world offers. It isn't determined by circumstances or dependent on what's happening outside us. It comes from the inside and has its basis in God.

Because God never changes, His joy never changes. It's always there within you, and it's always the same. Even when you're going through troubles and trials, the joy of the Lord can give you a wonderful sense of lightness. It can rise up within you and give you a supernatural gladness that lifts you above your natural circumstances.

Joy is a spiritual force that's born into you like the other fruit of the spirit. It springs out of your love and attention toward God. The more loving fellowship you have with Him, the more joy you'll walk in. Depending on how much living contact you have with Him in the Word and in prayer, joy will either trickle through your life in a tiny stream or rush through you like a mighty, roaring river.

Give Joy the Right of Way

Of course, even if you maintain a rich fellowship with the Lord, for the joy that's within you to flow freely, you have to yield to it. You have to respond like you do when you're driving your car. When you come to an intersection where there's a yield sign, if another car is there, you yield by letting the other car go first.

That's how it is with the fruit of the spirit. Your soul is the intersection, or crossroad, where your flesh and spirit meet. When a situation comes up and you're tempted to be downcast, rather than just giving in to that negative emotion, pause for a moment and give your spirit the right of way.

Resist the pull toward depression. Let joy take the lead by stirring it up in your spirit and connecting with the Lord.

Joy is in your heart. It's also in the presence of God. So, when you get those two locations together, joy becomes doubly powerful. It comes forth with enough force to overcome any tribulation or depression. The Bible says it's your strength (Nehemiah 8:10). As that force continues to flow, over time, it will permeate even your natural temperament. It will become a part of your outer man just as it's part of your inner man.

When that happens, your whole life will be positively affected! You'll be able to enjoy life more. You'll also be able to receive more easily from God. Why? Because as Isaiah 12:3 says: "With joy will you draw water from the wells of salvation" (AMPC).

Salvation isn't just the new birth. It includes healing and prosperity and all the other redemptive blessings of God. Those blessings are all yours in Jesus, but you don't draw them out with depression or down-heartedness. You draw them out with the joy of the Lord.

It's easy to receive healing in a service where the joy of the Lord is being manifested! I know because I've experienced it. I've been in services where people who were sick praised God and rejoiced in Him until holy laughter broke out. I've seen them celebrate God's greatness until they overflowed with such joy that the sickness in their bodies suddenly seemed like nothing at all. God got so big in their thinking, that drawing on His healing power became as simple as breathing, and they received their healing and went home well!

Joy can have the same effect when it comes to receiving things like pros-perity or divine wisdom. It will encourage your faith to the point where you find it easy to reach out and receive whatever blessings you need. Just as faith and love work together, faith and joy work together. Where being sad and discouraged pulls your faith down, joy strengthens it and causes it to rise.

As believers, we ought to live in a continual flow of the joy of the Lord! After all, we're the redeemed. We're the people about whom Isaiah prophesied:

> Therefore the redeemed of the Lord shall return, and come
> with singing unto Zion; and everlasting joy shall be upon

their head: they shall obtain gladness and joy; and sorrow and mourning shall flee away.... [And the Lord shall] give unto them beauty for ashes, the oil of joy for mourning, the garment of praise for the spirit of heaviness; that they might be called trees of righteousness, the planting of the Lord, that he might be glorified (Isaiah 51:11, 61:3).

Consider for a moment all the reasons we have to be full of joy: Through the new birth, we've passed from death into life. Jesus has paid the price for our forgiveness. He's brought us into union with Himself and made us His joint heirs. In Him, we're blessed beyond measure in the here and now, and we have a glorious eternal future ahead of us. Instead of being on our way to hell, we're on our way to heaven!

Just thinking about everything Jesus has done for us makes me want to do a little jig right now. It makes me literally want to dance!

Dancing is a great way to express the joy of the Lord. It's also a good thing to do when you're tempted to get depressed.

I remember one time, years ago, I was at my desk in our ministry office, and a young man on our staff came in and gave me a negative report. "So-and-so criticized you and Kenneth on the radio," he said, "and this other person has been bad-mouthing your ministry all around town." I don't like being criticized any more than anyone else. But what popped into my mind at that moment was what Jesus said in Matthew 5:11-12: "Blessed are ye, when men shall revile you, and persecute you, and shall say all manner of evil against you falsely, for my sake. Rejoice, and be exceeding glad: for great is your reward in heaven."

One meaning of the word *rejoice* is "to leap for joy." So, right there in my office, I jumped up and began to dance before the Lord. I'm sure the young man who'd brought me the bad news wondered, *What has gotten into this woman?* But I didn't care what he thought. I just kept dancing and rejoicing. Instead of getting sad, I got glad!

You can do the same thing. When the spirit of heaviness tries to come on you, you can cast it off like someone else's old coat.

Speak Your Faith

You sad spirit, you get away from me! You're part of the old man, and I'm not wearing you for one moment. I choose to put on the new man (Ephesians 4:24). I receive the oil of joy for mourning, and I choose to put on the garment of praise for the spirit of heaviness (Isaiah 61:3). I choose to clothe myself with the garment of praise!

Living on the Joyful Side of the Cross

"But is it really possible for us to rejoice all the time?" you might ask. "Isn't Jesus sometimes saying to us, like He said to the disciples in John 16:22, 'Ye now therefore have sorrow'?"

No, He isn't! The only time Jesus said that was when He was talking to His disciples about leaving them and going to the cross. When He talked to them about what their life would be like after He went to the Cross, He said, "I will see you again and your heart will rejoice, and your joy no one will take from you" (verse 22, NKJV).

You and I are living on the joyful side of the Cross! We have a joy that can't be stolen by anyone. Because Jesus has risen and we've been redeemed, our hearts can rejoice continually.

It's important to note though, Jesus said it's our hearts that rejoice. It's not our heads or our emotions or our bodies that produce joy. Joy comes from the inward man. As we yield to and express the joy of the Lord that's on the inside, it flows outward and, in turn, will affect our heads, our emotions and our bodies. It fills us head to toe with a joy no man can give us, and none can take away!

Ken and I see this demonstrated all the time in our prison ministry. We constantly receive joyful testimonies from inmates who've received Jesus as Savior and Lord and learned about the Word of God by watching our television broadcast. They write to tell us that their hearts are rejoicing even though physically they're still behind bars. As one inmate told Ken, "Since I met Jesus, I'm freer inside this prison than I ever was on the outside!"

I know what he means. Although I've never been locked up in a literal prison, when Ken and I first started learning how to live by faith, we'd been locked up for years in financial lack. We were facing a mountain of debt that, despite our best efforts, had kept getting bigger instead of smaller. We had no money in the bank and barely enough income to live on.

We'd moved to Tulsa so that Ken could be a student at Oral Roberts University, and we were living in an absolutely awful little house. It had brown paint peeling from the walls and it was so bad, I refused to unpack for two weeks. Ken was preaching out of town a lot, and we couldn't afford for me to go with him. I didn't have any money to go shopping or other places, so I spent most of my days in that dingy, little house taking care of our young children.

In the natural, it didn't look like I had much going for me. But I wasn't in the natural. I was in the Word! I was just beginning to find out what belonged to me in Jesus, and I was spending every spare moment reading my Bible and listening to cassette tapes on faith by Kenneth E. Hagin. Almost everything he was preaching was new to me, and I was so eager to absorb it, I took pages of notes on every message. I think I eventually wrote down almost everything he said!

I'd get so excited listening to those tapes and reading the Word that sometimes I'd hardly know what to do. I just wanted to get up and run around the room because the joy of the Lord was being so stirred up inside me.

Before long, that joy pretty much took over my life. It flowed out of me so naturally that one day when I was outside hanging clothes on the clothesline, I ran inside to answer the phone. Instead of saying hello, I said, "Hallelujah!" It just came out of me because I was so full of the joy of the Lord!

This is how God intends for believers to live. He doesn't want us to have just a little bit of joy. He doesn't want just a little to leak out of us every once in a while. He wants fullness of joy flowing out of us all the time. That's one of the reasons He tells us to stay full of the Word.

Our Word level and our joy level are directly connected.

Jesus said in John 15:11, "These things have I spoken unto you, that my joy might remain in you, and that your joy might be full." Jeremiah 15:16 says, "Thy words were found, and I did eat them; and thy word was unto me the joy and rejoicing of mine heart."

That's what happened to me during those early days in Tulsa! I found and fed on God's Word, and my heart was rejoicing. I wasn't worried anymore about having to live in that tacky little house. I wasn't depressed because we didn't have money and I had holes in my shoes. I'd fallen in love with God. I'd heard and believed His good Word, and I was on top of the world!

Today, more than 50 years later, I'm still on top of the world! I'm still finding and believing God's Word, and it's still bringing me joy. I'm more in love with the Lord now than ever, and I can certainly confirm what Alexander Maclaren wrote:

> There is only one source of permanent joy which takes posses-
> sion of and fills all the corners and crannies of the heart, and
> that is a love toward God.... If God is "the gladness of our joy"

and all our delights come from communion with Him, our joy will never pass....[9]

One of the problems with natural happiness is that, unlike the joy of the Lord, natural happiness is always fleeting. It can bring gladness and pleasure for a short while, but because it's based on earthly circumstances, its delight never lasts. You might dream about getting a new car, for example. When you buy it, though you're momentarily happy as you drive it off the car lot, after a while, that car doesn't give you the thrill you thought it would. You might continue to like it and be glad you have it, but it won't give you lasting joy. Joy doesn't come from material things or earthly circumstances. True joy comes only from the Word and fellowship with the Lord.

Power to Overcome

Another marvelous benefit of joy is its ability to fortify our inner man. As Nehemiah 8:10 says, "The joy of the Lord is your strength." When things get tough, if you're walking in joy, you don't get weak and quit. You keep marching forward in triumph and finish what God has called you to do.

"...Power to overcome is joy's main attribute," says Greg Zoschack. "...Thus there are three functions of the fruit of joy: 1) To produce victory, 2) To provide fulfillment, 3) To protect against oppression.... In essence, *joy is a preventative fruit that protects against falling into bondage and servitude to the enemy of God.*"[10] Its strength enables a person to remain steadfast.

When you have the joy of the Lord working in you, you can keep looking to Him in the midst of bad circumstances. You can maintain

---

9   Maclaren, "Galatians v. 22, 23, The Fruit of the Spirit," in *Expositions of Holy Scripture.*

10   Zoschak, *A Call for Character,* 47, 48, 50.

your walk with God and stay strong in faith until your breakthrough comes. That's why James 1 says:

> Consider it wholly joyful, my brethren, whenever you are enveloped in or encounter trials of any sort or fall into various temptations. Be assured and understand that the trial and proving of your faith bring out endurance and steadfastness and patience. But let endurance and steadfastness and patience have full play and do a thorough work, so that you may be [people] perfectly and fully developed [with no defects], lacking in nothing (verses 2-4, AMPC).

"Gloria," you might say, "sometimes, when circumstances are really bad, I can't count it all joy. Sometimes, I don't have any reasons to rejoice."

Sure, you do! For one thing, you can rejoice that you're not in those circumstances alone. You're not just wandering around helplessly in the dark like you were back when you were in the world. Back then, you didn't have any answers. You didn't have Jesus and His supernatural overcoming power to depend on. You didn't have the Word or any divine wisdom to guide you to victory. All you had was what the natural world could do for you—and that wasn't much!

Now that you're in God, when you go through tests and trials, you have a lot more options. You're not limited to what you see with your eyes. You don't have to rely just on the information your physical senses provide. You're a born-again spirit. You have tremendous advantages. You can live in a way that people who aren't born again cannot.

Because the Holy Spirit is in you, you have the answer to every problem!

God not only knows the answer to every situation you could ever face, He promised to *give you* that answer. He said in James 1:5, "If any of you lack wisdom, let him ask of God, that giveth to all men liberally, and upbraideth not; and it shall be given him."

The AMPC says, "If any of you is deficient in wisdom, let him ask of the giving God [Who gives] to everyone liberally and ungrudgingly, without reproaching or faultfinding, and it will be given him." And, the NLT says, "If you need wisdom, ask our generous God, and he will give it to you. He will not rebuke you for asking."

God is so wonderful that even when you're facing a problem that's a result of your own mistakes, He won't upbraid (find fault with) you. He won't say things like, "Well, you got yourself into this mess, you get yourself out. You made your bed hard, now you lie in it."

People might say those kinds of things, but God won't. He's not like that.

He set up the plan of Redemption so that if you do sin and get yourself into a bad situation, when you repent, the blood of Jesus will cleanse you of all unrighteousness. You can receive your forgiveness by faith and say, "Father, show me the way out. Show me what I need to do here."

When you do that, He'll always reveal to you a course of action. He'll give you wisdom from heaven that will turn things around.

There is one caveat, though: To receive God's wisdom, you have to "ask in faith, nothing wavering. For he that wavereth is like a wave of the sea driven with the wind and tossed. For let not that man think that he shall receive any thing of the Lord. A double minded man is unstable in all his ways" (verses 6-8).

Praying in faith means you believe you receive the moment you ask and, from then on, you speak accordingly. You don't go out of your prayer place wringing your hands and saying, "I just don't know what I'm going to do. I'm doomed. I'm going to die. I'm going to go bankrupt."

Speak Your Faith

I have the wisdom of God and the mind of Christ. My wonderful heavenly Father gives me the answers I need to overcome every temptation and trial with joy. I'm going to come out of this. I'll not die, but live and declare the works of the Lord. I'll not go bankrupt. I will walk in God's blessings and prosper. I choose to rejoice because Jesus took my sicknesses and pain, and by His stripes, I was already healed 2,000 years ago (1 Peter 2:24)! I choose to rejoice because my God supplies all my need according to His riches in glory by Christ Jesus (Philippians 4:19). I am an overcomer in every area of my life because greater is He who is in me than he who is in the world (1 John 4:4)!

This is how you keep yourself open to hear from heaven. You stand on the Word of God, stay stable in faith, and don't waver.

"But what if the answer doesn't come for a while?"

Just keep counting it all joy and believing God. If you'll do that, you're sure to end up in victory because believing and rejoicing work together. Believing what God says in His Word causes you to rejoice, and rejoicing reinforces your faith and keeps it strong. Greg Zoschak said, "A Christian's faith will never rise above his joy, and his joy will never rise above his faith."[11]

Faith and joy stand together on the solid foundation of God's Word. As the Bible says:

> ...believing, ye rejoice with joy unspeakable and full of glory: receiving the end of your faith, even the salvation of your souls (1 Peter 1:8-9).

---

11 Zoschak, *A Call for Character,* 59.

The God of hope fill you with all joy and peace in believing, that ye may abound in hope, through the power of the Holy Ghost (Romans 15:13).

And having this confidence, I know that I shall abide and continue with you all for your furtherance and joy of faith; that your rejoicing may be more abundant in Jesus Christ... (Philippians 1:25-26).

Keep Rejoicing, and Don't Fret

Jerry Savelle said this years ago: "If Satan can't steal your joy, he can't keep your goods."[12] That's the absolute truth! The devil can't whip you and neither can anyone else because you're walking in the supernatural force of victory that "overcometh the world" (1 John 5:4).

If you're in joy, you're in faith; and if you're in faith, you're totally unbeatable.

It's no wonder God made rejoicing a scriptural command! It's no wonder He said in Philippians 4:

Rejoice in the Lord always [delight, gladden yourselves in Him]; again I say, Rejoice!... Do not fret or have any anxiety about anything, but in every circumstance and in everything, by prayer and petition (definite requests), with thanksgiving, continue to make your wants known to God (verses 4, 6, AMPC).

According to those verses, if you're depressed and in sorrow, you're not being scriptural. To be scriptural you must *rejoice always*. You must constantly gladden yourself in the Lord and refuse to fret.

---

12   Jerry Savelle, *If Satan Can't Steal Your Joy...He Can't Keep Your Goods* (Tulsa: Harrison House Inc., 2002).

What exactly is *fret?*

It's worry. It's an anxious state of mind that arises when you anticipate a negative outcome. When your child does something wrong and you think, *Oh my! That child is going to keep getting in worse and worse trouble,* that's fretting. When you watch the news and say, "Those dumb politicians are going to raise my taxes until I go broke!" that's fretting.

These days, especially, you have to be selective about how much news you watch. The media is broadcasting 24 hours a day, and they always have something bad to report. Listening to too much of that will eventually cause you to fret. So, shut it off sometimes, and read the Word instead. Set your mind on the Lord, and pray about those things that need to be fixed in this country instead of worrying about what the commentators are saying about them.

Worrying won't help, anyway. It will only make the situation worse. So rather than being part of the problem, become part of the solution. Where this nation and current events are concerned, lift them before God, believe Him and rejoice!

If you do watch the news, use words of faith to combat the darkness and the negative thoughts it tries to inject into you. Talk back to the television. If a newscaster says something that tries to steal your joy or your faith, speak your faith out loud instead. Refuse to receive a bad report about this country or anything else! Declare instead that Jesus is Lord over your life and this country, and that it's not going down into ungodliness. It's awakening to God!

Take the same attitude when you're faced with some kind of bad news in your personal life. When a problem crops up in your family, church or business, instead of fretting about it, take it to the throne of grace. Pray about it, leave it with God, and then keep the switch of faith turned on. Rejoice in the victory by faith, *before* you see the manifestation. Let the force of joy sustain you.

Faith is what gets your prayers answered. Fretting just gets in the way. So, once you've prayed, strengthen your faith by rejoicing, and if fret tries to come on you again, turn it away.

Then rebuke thoughts of fear and replace them with gratitude.

Speak Your Faith

I've already put this problem into the hands of the Lord, and He's seeing to it. It's not my problem anymore. It's God's, and He is well able to handle it!

Thank You, Lord, that You are causing all things to work together for my good. Thank You that I'm healed and prospering. I'm so thankful, Lord. I rejoice in all the good things You're doing in my life!

Praise Opens Prison Doors

The Apostle Paul is a good example of what it looks like to live this kind of faith-filled, joyful lifestyle. He rejoiced even in the midst of the most trying situations. And, as we've already seen, he faced a lot of them!

He encountered almost constant persecution from the religious people who resented his ministry. More than once, he even wound up literally being thrown out of the cities where he was preaching. It's not very much fun to get thrown out of a place—especially when you're just trying to bless people and obey God. Yet, when it happened to Paul, he responded by continuing to share the gospel and staying "filled with joy, and with the Holy Ghost" (Acts 13:52).

Paul practiced what he preached! He rejoiced always, no matter how bad his circumstances were.

On one occasion, Paul found himself in dire straits because he cast a devil out of a young slave girl who had been making a great deal of money for her masters by telling fortunes. When the demon left, the girl lost her fortune-telling ability. That made her masters mad, so they dragged Paul and Silas before the rulers of the city and accused them of being troublemakers:

> And the multitude rose up together against them: and the magistrates rent off their clothes, and commanded to beat them. And when they had laid many stripes upon them, they cast them into prison, charging the jailor to keep them safely: who, having received such a charge, thrust them into the inner prison, and made their feet fast in the stocks (Acts 16:22-24).

If anyone ever had a good excuse to be depressed, Paul and Silas did right there! They could have totally lost their joy in that situation. Silas could have said, "Paul, we're in this prison because of you! You missed God when you decided we should come here. If you hadn't led us into this, we'd still be free!"

Paul could have given in to self-pity and thought, *Surely God will understand if I cry and get a little sad here for a while. Surely, He doesn't expect me to be joyful while I'm bleeding and bruised, behind bars and locked up in these stocks.*

But that's not the attitude Paul and Silas chose to take. They didn't moan and groan and weep over their predicament. They didn't say, "God, why did You let this happen to us?" They remained joyful.

> And at midnight Paul and Silas prayed, and sang praises unto God: and the prisoners heard them. And suddenly there was a great earthquake, so that the foundations of the prison were ̌aken: and immediately all the doors were opened, and every ̌e's bands were loosed (verses 25-26).

If Paul and Silas had let the devil steal their joy, there wouldn't have been any supernatural earthquake that night. If they'd just cried and had a pity party, the prison would have stayed locked up tight. But Paul and Silas refused to let that situation get them down. They sang praises even in that hard situation, and God supernaturally set them free.

What's more, after the earthquake, the jailer came rushing in to see what had happened. Realizing it had been an act of God, trembling with fear, he asked Paul and Silas how to be saved (verses 29-30). They preached the gospel to him, and even more joy broke out because he "rejoiced, believing in God with all his house" (verse 34).

Paul and Silas had quite a time that day! They let the joy of the Lord be their strength, and they overcame. They not only walked out of that prison, they did what they were divinely called to do, and there were a number of souls added to the kingdom of God!

This is the way Paul lived his whole life. Even though he faced bonds and afflictions everywhere he preached, he said, "None of these things move me, neither count I my life dear unto myself, so that I might finish my course *with joy,* and the ministry, which I have received of the Lord Jesus, to testify the gospel of the grace of God" (Acts 20:24).

The words *with joy* give us great insight into how Paul was able to fulfill the massive mission Jesus had given him. He did it by walking in joy. That's how you'll finish your mission, too! As you keep yielding to joy, you'll continually be strengthened and empowered to live in a way that's pleasing to God and advances His kingdom.

Paul wrote this in Romans 14:17-18: "The kingdom of God is...righteousness, and peace, and joy in the Holy Ghost. For he that in these things serveth Christ is acceptable to God, *and approved of men.*" So, joy will also help you finish your course by giving you favor with people. When you're walking in love and joy, they'll want to be in your presence. They'll feel good when you're around, and they'll want to do things to help you.

That's what happened with the Philippian jailer who rescued Paul and Silas that night. He favored them to such a degree that he not only let them out of prison, he took them home with him. He even washed their wounds and fed them dinner!

Think about that. Paul and Silas' joy and rejoicing opened the door for that jailer's attitude toward them to be totally transformed. Their praises put the devil to flight, and the jailer went from being their captor to being their liberator. He went from being their enemy to being their spiritual brother and friend.

> *Joyful praise brings the presence of the Lord on the scene and causes the devil to flee.*

It defeats our spiritual enemy. But lack of joy does just the opposite. It leaves us in bondage. It puts us in the position God warned the Israelites about when He said, "Because thou servedst not the Lord thy God with joyfulness, and with gladness of heart, for the abundance of all things; therefore shalt thou serve thine enemies..." (Deuteronomy 28:47-48).

You don't want to end up serving your enemies! You want to keep rejoicing and praising and thanking God, even in the worst situations. You want to be like the psalmist who wrote, "I will be glad and rejoice in thee: I will sing praise to thy name, O thou most High. When mine enemies are turned back, they shall fall and perish at thy presence" (Psalm 9:2-3).

If you'll take that attitude, God can do for you what He did when He delivered the Israelites from captivity in Egypt. Psalm 105:43 says, "He brought forth his people with joy, and his chosen with gladness." Verse 37 says, "He brought them forth also with silver and gold: and there was not one feeble person among their tribes."

Regardless of how crazy things get in this world, as a believer, you never have to be depressed, sad or discouraged. You can go around all the time with a smile on your face. You can rejoice and be happy simply because joy is part of your spiritual inheritance. God has provided it for you in abundance, and you can tap into it whenever you want. All you have to do is spend time in fellowship with Him and declare, as people of God did throughout the Scriptures:

Thou hast put gladness in my heart (Psalm 4:7).

And my soul shall be joyful in the Lord: it shall rejoice in his salvation (Psalm 35:9).

Then will I go unto the altar of God, unto God my exceeding joy: yea...will I praise thee, O God my God (Psalm 43:4).

My spirit hath rejoiced in God my Saviour (Luke 1:47).

And not only so, but we also joy in God through our Lord Jesus Christ, by whom we have now received the atonement (Romans 5:11).

Rejoicing is a choice! So, when you get up and have your prayer time every morning, be joyful on purpose. Praise and worship God for all the things He's done in your life. Get up and dance before Him. Thank Him for sending Jesus to pay the price for you. Thank Him for all the times He's healed your body. Thank Him for your family and your friends. Thank Him for the things He's promised and you're believing for but haven't yet seen with your natural eyes. See those things done with the eyes of your spirit, and rejoice over them.

Make joy a lifestyle. Make it a daily habit. Even in your darkest hours, when natural circumstances threaten to imprison you, talk back to them.

Speak Your Faith

"Yet I will rejoice in the Lord, I will joy in the God of my salvation" (Habakkuk 3:18). I'm not moved by what I see. I'm not moved by what I hear. I'm only moved by the Word of God, and He always causes me to triumph (2 Corinthians 2:14). I choose to thank and praise and worship God. I choose joy!

Now watch those prison doors fly open, and you'll go free!

Chapter 9

PEACE LIKE A RIVER

*And suddenly there was with the angel a multitude of the
heavenly host praising God, and saying, Glory to God in
the highest, and on earth peace, good will toward men.*

LUKE 2:13-14

The fruit of the spirit are powerful, and all of them have been given by
God to protect you from the attacks of Satan and enable you to live
in victory. Yet there's one fruit in particular that holds a very special place
in the Bible. This one is so closely associated with the coming of Jesus that
on the day of His birth, the angels announced its restoration to mankind.

What is it? It's the force of *peace.*

Peace is wonderful! It's something every person on earth desperately
desires and, like love and joy, it can only be found in God.

Peace is the aspect of God's nature that can be described as "a sustained state of quietness, calmness, tranquility and absence of strife." It
flows into us through our fellowship with God and then comes out of us
so that other people get to enjoy it.

The divine force of peace can give you a sense of well-being even when all your circumstances are turned upside down and everything seems to be going wrong. It can enable you to remain undisturbed even in the midst of a crisis situation. God's peace "surpasses all understanding" (Philippians 4:7, NKJV), and can neither be produced nor comprehended by the world because it's not based on what's happening in this natural realm. It's based on the knowledge that your relationship with God is intact. It comes from knowing that He loves you, is taking care of you, and is working on your behalf.

The Greek word translated *peace* in the New Testament literally means "to bind or join together that which has been separated," and it perfectly describes what happens to believers through the new birth. We've been joined together with God. We're no longer separated from Him by sin. He's become our heavenly Father, and we've become His beloved children, eternally united with Him by our faith in Jesus as our Redeemer and Lord.

That's what the angels were rejoicing about in Bethlehem!

When they said to the shepherds, "Peace on earth, good will toward men," they weren't talking about peace between people. They weren't just telling us to express goodwill toward one another. They were talking about goodwill between God and mankind. They were saying that because God had sent Jesus, the Christ, the Messiah, as a Savior to the world, we can have peace with God.

Peace is really what Jesus' ministry was all about. It was so central to His mission that, in the Scriptures, it's included as part of His Name. As Isaiah 9:6 says, "For unto us a child is born, unto us a son is given...and his name shall be called Wonderful, Counsellor, The mighty God, The everlasting Father, *The Prince of Peace.*"

A New Testament Greek lexicon says, "This state [of peace] is the object of divine and saving promise, and is brought about by God's mercy, granting deliverance and freedom from all distresses that are experienced as the result of sin."[13]

Alexander Maclaren wrote, "Peace will be built upon love and joy, if our hearts are ever turning to God and ever blessed with the inter-communion of love between Him and us.... True peace comes not from the absence of trouble but from the presence of God, and will be deep and passing all understanding in the exact measure in which we live in, and partake of, the love of God."[14]

This is why the message of salvation is called the gospel (or good news) of peace! When you believe that Jesus paid the price for *all* sin, your sins can't keep you out of God's presence any longer. You're free to draw near to Him and partake of all the riches of His Redemption.

When you live in constant fellowship with Him, you can receive from Him everything you need to live in peace.

"Well," someone might say, "all we really need to live in peace is to know we're going to heaven when we die, isn't it?"

No, that's where peace starts, but there's so much more to it. It is *everything which makes for a man's highest good.*

It doesn't make for your highest good to have sickness or disease in your body. It doesn't make for your highest good to be in lack and unable to put food on your table or buy clothes for your children. It doesn't make for your highest good to be worried and tormented in your mind. So, when God sent Jesus to be our Peace, He delivered us from those negative conditions by taking them on Himself. As Isaiah 53 says:

---

13   Hermann Cremer, *Biblico-Theological Lexicon of New Testament Greek,* trans. D.W. Simon, W. Urwick (T. & T. Clark: Edinburgh, 1872) p. 226.

14   Maclaren, "Galatians: The Fruit of the Spirit," in *Expositions of Holy Scripture.*

Surely He has borne our griefs (sicknesses, weaknesses, and distresses) and carried our sorrows and pains [of punishment].... He was wounded for our transgressions, He was bruised for our guilt and iniquities; the chastisement [needful to obtain] peace and well-being for us was upon Him, and with the stripes [that wounded] Him we are healed and made whole (verses 4-5, AMPC).

Jesus did more than just secure you a place in heaven when He went to the cross. He paid the price for your complete peace. He provided for you everything that makes for your highest good—spirit, soul, body, relationally and financially!

He bore your sin so that you could "become the righteousness of God in Him" (2 Corinthians 5:21, NKJV).

He bore all your sicknesses and pains so that you can receive healing and live in divine health.

He bore all the grief, agitation, depression, anxiety, fear and oppression that could ever come against your mind, and suffered with them in your place so that no matter what your circumstances, you can walk all the time in perfect mental and emotional peace.

Wow, I'm Glad That Person Is Here!

Peace is, and always has been, God's will for people. It was even His will before Jesus came. All through the Old Testament, God gave the Israelites His Word and told them how to have peace in their lives. He promised that if they'd obey Him, they'd prosper in every way and even have peace with other nations. No enemy would be able to stand against them.

Much of the time, though, the Israelites refused to obey Him. They forfeited their peace by ignoring His instructions and going their own way. Yet even when they rebelled, God refused to give up on them. He kept calling them back to Himself and saying, as He did through Isaiah:

> Thus saith the Lord, thy Redeemer, the Holy One of Israel; I am the Lord thy God which teacheth thee to profit, which leadeth thee by the way that thou shouldest go. O that thou hadst hearkened to my commandments! then had thy peace been as a river, and thy righteousness as the waves of the sea (Isaiah 48:17-18).

Notice those verses compare peace to a river. A well-supplied river never runs dry. It's always producing an outflow.

That's the way God wants His peace to be in the lives of His people. He doesn't want us to bring strife into situations. He doesn't want us to bring in turmoil, upset and anxiety. He wants us to have such an overflowing supply of peace that it continually pours out of our spirits into the environment around us. He wants us to be so flooded with it that no matter how seemingly disturbing the circumstances might be, when we arrive on the scene everyone thinks, *Wow! I'm glad that person is here!*

What's the secret to having that much peace? How do we cultivate it so that, even when we find ourselves surrounded by trouble, we bring peace with us wherever we go? Isaiah 26:3 tells us: "Thou wilt keep him in perfect peace, whose mind is stayed on thee: because he trusteth in thee."

Peace comes from keeping your attention on God! It's fueled by your faith in Him. If you keep your mind on Him and His Word, your peace will keep flowing.

If you allow yourself to get distracted by contrary circumstances, on the other hand, your river of peace will begin to dry up. The devil will get your ear and start talking to you about how bad things look. He'll flash negative pictures across your mind. He'll tell you God is not going to come through for you this time and, before you know it, you'll be anxious and upset.

Rather than trusting God to take care of you, rebuking those thoughts of unbelief and telling them to get out, you'll be wondering why God let you get into this situation in the first place. You'll be envisioning what a terrible disaster it might turn out to be and thinking thoughts of defeat instead of victory. Your peace will be replaced by worry—all because somewhere along the way, you got your mind off God and stopped believing what He said in the Scriptures.

"But Gloria, sometimes the situations I'm facing are really serious! I can't stop worrying about them altogether!"

Yes, you can. The Lord commands you to do so. He says in Philippians 4:6-8, AMPC:

> Do not fret or have any anxiety about anything, but in every circumstance and in everything, by prayer and petition (definite requests), with thanksgiving, continue to make your wants known to God. And God's peace [shall be yours, that tranquil state of a soul assured of its salvation through Christ, and so fearing nothing from God and being content with its earthly lot of whatever sort that is, that peace] which transcends all understanding shall garrison and mount guard over your hearts and minds in Christ Jesus. For the rest, brethren, whatever is true, whatever is worthy of reverence and is honorable and seemly, whatever is just, whatever is pure, whatever is lovely and lovable, whatever is kind and winsome and gracious, if there is any virtue and excellence, if there is anything worthy of praise, think on and weigh and take account of these things [fix your minds on them].

Those verses make it clear that what you think about is your responsibility. You don't have to just accept every disturbing, fearful and unbelieving thought the devil tries to sell you. You can keep your mind continually filled with thoughts about the goodness and faithfulness of God.

His peace will rise up strongly in you as you think about Him, His blessings and His exceeding great and precious promises.

It will hold you steady through every test or trial until the answer from heaven arrives. Joshua proved this in the Old Testament. He had to go through many trials and troubles when he took the Israelites into the Promised Land. He had to stay steady in the face of seemingly unwinnable battles. There were cities with massive walls around them that he had to overcome. And Joshua had to battle armies made up of men who were literally giants. Beside that, he had to lead a nation of several million people. How did he maintain his peace through it all?

Before he went into the land, God told him the secret. He said, "Joshua, think about My Word all the time. Talk about it and meditate on it day and night. Then you'll do it, and it will cause you to prosper and have good success."[15]

Those weren't necessarily easy instructions for Joshua to follow. But he obeyed them anyway. He kept his attention on God's Word and stayed in faith until God's promises were fulfilled in his life.

If Joshua could do that under the old covenant, we can do it today under the new covenant which is based on better promises (Hebrews 8:6)!

We not only have the written Word of God, we have the Spirit of Jesus Christ living inside us, and He's given us His own peace.

---

15   See Joshua 1:8.

That peace is one of Redemption's greatest gifts! Jesus considered it to be so valuable and important that it's one of the last things He talked about before He went to the cross. Just hours before His death, He said to His disciples, "Peace I leave with you, my peace I give unto you: not as the world giveth, give I unto you. Let not your heart be troubled, neither let it be afraid" (John 14:27).

Oh, what a powerful and precious gift Jesus bestowed on us as believers when He gave us His peace! It will keep us calm and give us a sense of well-being, even at times when trouble and danger are bearing down on us. It will work together with our faith to preserve us as we look to the Word to bring us out.

No matter how big a problem you may be facing, there *is* a way out. There *is* an answer to it with God, and as you draw near to Him, He'll give it to you. As you keep your mind on what He says and refuse to be troubled, He'll give you His perspective on the situation. He'll show you what to say and what to do, and as you do it, just like Joshua 1:8 says, "...you will make your way prosperous, and then you will have good success" (NKJV).

No Exceptions. No Exclusions.

"But my biggest problems are with my children!" someone might say. "They've strayed from God. They're living a lifestyle that puts them in danger. Surely Jesus doesn't expect me to be calm and peaceful in the face of that!"

Yes, He does. He didn't mention any exceptions or exclusions when He told us to not worry. He said, "Let not your heart be troubled." Period. So, you don't even have to let the situations involving your children rob you of your peace.

You can do everything you know to do for your children in the natural, and then trust God with them. You can pray for their salvation and deliverance, cast the care of them over on God, and lock onto scriptures like those in Isaiah 54 where God said:

> And all thy children shall be taught of the Lord; and great shall be the peace of thy children. In righteousness shalt thou be established: thou shalt be far from oppression; for thou shalt not fear: and from terror; for it shall not come near thee.... No weapon that is formed against thee shall prosper; and every tongue that shall rise against thee in judgment thou shalt condemn. This is the heritage of the servants of the Lord, and their righteousness is of me, saith the Lord (verses 13-14, 17).

As a believer, those verses belong to you! They were given to you by God to stand on in faith. So take them as your own, and believe God for your children. Find out what else the Word says about them, and declare it over them. Practice thinking about them and seeing them in the light of the Scriptures.

If things look bad in your children's lives right now, don't think about them as they are in the natural. If you do, they'll stay that way, and that's not what you want. You want to change what's happening in their lives. Keep the switch of faith turned on. Faith doesn't look at circumstances, it looks at the Word of God. So, keep your focus there.

Speak Your Faith

I refuse to receive those negative thoughts about my children! I see my son whole and living in righteousness. I see my daughter saved, serving God and in peace. I see them, and their children, as disciples, taught of the Lord, obedient to His will, and great is their peace and undisturbed composure (Isaiah 54:13, AMPC).

Don't let the devil distract you from the promises God has given you about your children by getting you over into anxiety. Don't let him undermine your faith with fear. He'll try to bring you mental pictures of your children getting into trouble or on drugs or going to prison, but push those thoughts away.

I realize it can sometimes be difficult to see them that way. I've been there! Many years ago, when my son, John, was a teenager, he really challenged me in this area. He was adventurous to the point of being reckless, and he kept doing things Ken and I didn't want him to do that would get him into trouble. He liked to drive fast, and it seemed he was perpetually turning over a truck, a motorcycle or some other kind of vehicle.

I diligently prayed and believed God to protect him. I stood on the Word and endeavored to stay in peace where he was concerned. But because he was making choices that opened the door to the devil, I was concerned he wouldn't live long enough for what God promised to come to pass in his life!

One day, when Ken and I were on an airplane in Australia on a ministry trip, I got particularly disturbed about John. Thoughts of him being killed in an accident flashed across my mind, and I knew the devil was trying to steal my faith. Ken was sitting beside me on the plane, and though I didn't tell him what I was thinking, right at that moment, he turned to me and said, "The Lord just spoke to me. He said, *My mercy hovers over John.*"

That was a direct answer from heaven to the anxiety I felt at that moment. It was God's word to me, and it has stayed with me and from that day to this. Even after John grew up and became the executive head of our ministry, whenever he had to go places where he might be in danger, those words resounded in my spirit: *My mercy hovers over John.*

God is saying the same thing to you about your children. He said it to all of us. He declared it in Psalm 145:9: "The Lord is good to all: and his tender mercies are over all his works."

If you'll believe that, instead of believing the devil's report and negative things you sometimes see, the peace of God will mount guard over your heart where your children and/or your grandchildren are concerned. You'll be able to maintain your stand of faith and keep the door open for God to fulfill what He said about them in His Word. I'm telling you, God is well able to take care of your children and grandchildren.

It doesn't matter how far afield your children or grandchildren might wander, He can get them back on track again!

God even said in Zechariah 10:8 that He will "hiss for them, and gather them" to Himself. The word *hiss* means "to signal or whistle for someone to come." It paints the picture of God flagging down that boy or girl of yours who's been out there doing the wrong thing. It shows Him whistling for them, to get their attention, and bringing them back into His will.

Believe God to do that for your children! Stop worrying about them, and pray in faith for Him to send laborers across their path. He has people they'll listen to, and if you'll ask Him, He'll put those people in the right place at the right time. As you keep trusting Him and refusing to worry, He'll save and deliver your children. He'll cause things to turn out for you and for them that are according to His plan:

> For I know the thoughts and plans that I have for you, says the Lord, thoughts and plans for welfare and peace and not for evil, to give you hope in your final outcome (Jeremiah 29:11, AMPC).

Let Peace Be Your Umpire

In addition to a sense of calmness and well-being, peace also provides us with another powerful benefit: It helps us discern the will of God so we can make wise decisions.

I discovered this when I first began walking with the Lord. I was reading my AMPC one day, and I came across Colossians 3:15:

> Let the peace (soul harmony which comes) from Christ rule (act as umpire continually) in your hearts [deciding and settling with finality all questions that arise in your minds, in that peaceful state] to which as [members of Christ's] one body you were also called [to live]. And be thankful (appreciative), [giving praise to God always].

As a brand-new believer, I got excited about that scripture. It really helped me. I wanted with all my heart to do the will of God and hadn't yet heard any teaching about being led by the Holy Spirit. I began to practice letting the peace of God lead me. I began to let it show me which way to go and what I should do or not do in certain situations.

I still live that way today, more than 50 years later. Having learned that peace is one of the primary signs of the Holy Spirit's leading, I continue to look to it to guide me. When I'm presented with an opportunity, and I'm not sure whether it's of God, I'll stop and ask myself, *What do I sense in my heart about this? It sounds like a good thing. It looks like a reasonable and intelligent option. But do I have peace about it? Or do I have more peace about doing something else?*

If I don't know the answer, I wait for a while and inquire of the Lord. I pray, watch over my heart and weigh the different options. For a while, I might be indecisive about the matter. As I consider various alternatives and seek the Lord about which one He wants me to choose, I might lean toward doing one thing one day and another thing the next.

When it comes to ministry matters, this probably frustrates our staff sometimes. But I won't finalize any important decision until I have peace about it. And on occasion, getting to that place takes time. When it does, I can't force it or hurry it up. I just have to keep looking to the Lord until peace decides and settles with finality all questions that arise in my mind.

In the meantime, I maintain my overall sense of calmness by doing what the rest of Colossians 3:15 says: "Be thankful (appreciative), [giving praise to God always]" (AMPC).

Being thankful helps you maintain your peace even when you don't yet know what to do about a situation.

It helps ward off worry and anxiety. So when you're seeking direction from the Lord, make sure you stay in in a mode of thanksgiving. In your times of prayer, instead of just focusing on what you want God to do for you, take time to express your gratitude to Him for what He's already done.

You might not be living in your dream home yet, but if you have a home at all, be thankful for it. You might not yet be driving the car you're believing for, but if you have a car at all, be grateful for it. Treat it like it's the best car in the world. Keep praising God for it and that will help you be patient and stay in peace while you're believing Him for something better.

What if you don't have a home or a car? Be thankful that you're born again! Be thankful that you're filled with the Holy Spirit. Quote back to God some of the wonderful promises He's given you in the Bible, and give Him praise.

One thing that always fills me with gratitude is just thinking back about what life was like before I knew the Lord. Back then I didn't have any answers to the problems I was facing. When trouble hit and I needed supernatural help, I didn't have the exceeding great and precious promises of God. All I had to depend on was what I could muster up in the natural.

Before you heard the gospel and received Jesus as Lord of your life, you were in the same pitiful situation. There was no way you could live in and follow peace because, as Ephesians 2:12-15 says:

> At that time ye were without Christ, being aliens from the commonwealth of Israel, and strangers from the covenants of promise, having no hope, and without God in the world: But now in Christ Jesus ye who sometimes were far off are made nigh by the blood of Christ. For he is our peace, who hath made both one, and hath broken down the middle wall of partition between us; having abolished in his flesh the enmity, even the law of commandments contained in ordinances; for to make in himself of twain one new man, so making peace.

If you ever have trouble thinking of reasons to give thanks and praise to God, you can find plenty right there in those verses! All you have to do is read them, and they'll remind you that because of what Jesus did for you, you're not wandering around in the darkness of this world without hope anymore. You're not a stranger to the covenants of God, left to fend for yourself and live under the thumb of the devil. You're one of God's covenant people! Your sins have been forgiven. You've been made a joint heir with Christ.

> And He came and preached peace to you who were afar off and to those who were near. For through Him we both have access by one Spirit to the Father. Now, therefore, you are no longer strangers and foreigners, but fellow citizens with the saints and members of the household of God, having been built on the foundation of the apostles and prophets, Jesus Christ Himself being the chief cornerstone, in whom the whole building, being fitted together, grows into a holy

temple in the Lord, in whom you also are being built together for a dwelling place of God in the Spirit (Ephesians 2:17-22, NKJV).

Peaceable Habitations

Just think about what a blessing it is to be a dwelling place of God! As His dwelling place, you don't have to strive and struggle to find peace like the lost people do because you already have it. You have within you God's own supernatural peace.

You may not have yielded to that peace as much as you could, but it's in you. And it's not just there to be available every now and then if you want it. It's there because the Lord wants you to walk in it all the time. It's there because His will is for you to live continually in peace.

The Bible says it clearly:

God hath called us to peace (1 Corinthians 7:15).

Follow peace with all men, and holiness, without which no man shall see the Lord: looking diligently lest any man fail of the grace of God; lest any root of bitterness springing up trouble you, and thereby many be defiled (Hebrews 12:14-15).

Wherefore, beloved...be diligent that ye may be found of him in peace, without spot, and blameless (2 Peter 3:14).

May grace (God's favor) and peace (which is perfect well-being, all necessary good, all spiritual prosperity, and freedom from fears and agitating passions and moral conflicts) be multiplied to you in [the full, personal, precise, and correct] knowledge of God and of Jesus our Lord (2 Peter 1:2, AMPC).

Now the God of hope fill you with all joy and peace in believing (Romans 15:13).

Notice, those last two verses remind us that peace comes from knowing and believing God. It comes from attending to what He says to us in the Scriptures and in our hearts by the Holy Spirit.

God will tell you things that will save your life. He'll guide you in paths of peace. But for His guidance to do you any good, you must be alert and sensitive to it. You must listen to Him and be quick to obey Him. And you're only going to do that if you love and spend time in His Word. Peace and the Word are inseparably connected!

> *The more you esteem and attend to God's Word, the greater your peace will be.*[16]

The more you hear and heed God's voice, the more safety you'll dwell in, and the more secure you'll be.[17]

It's a wonderful thing these days to be able to live in security without fear of evil! These are troubled times. All around us in this world there's crime, violence and danger. In the natural, people don't have any assurance of protection. But as believers, we do! If we're walking in the spirit, we can stand in faith on God's promises, obey His directions, and expect our lives to line up with what He said in Isaiah 32:17-18:

> And the work of righteousness shall be peace; and the effect of righteousness quietness and assurance for ever. And my people shall dwell in a peaceable habitation, and in sure dwellings, and in quiet resting places.

I've seen God provide supernatural peace and protection in all kinds of situations over the years! I've seen Him do it in my own life, and I've

---

16   Psalm 119:165: "Great peace have they which love thy law."
17   Proverbs 1:33, NKJV: "Whoever listens to me will dwell safely, and will be secure, without fear of evil."

witnessed it time and again in the lives of others—sometimes in the midst of great turmoil and danger.

Take, for example, what He did back in 1994 for some friends of ours who were pastoring a church in Thousand Oaks, near Northridge, California. He started leading them just before the beginning of the year to teach their congregation about the protective power of the blood of Jesus. They didn't know why He was leading them that way. They'd just heard Billye Brim preach about the power of the blood here at Eagle Mountain International Church, and they got it in their hearts to preach the same series of messages at their own church.

The series continued for a number of weeks. At the end of the last message, the congregation all took Communion together and prayed over their homes. In the spirit, they put the blood of Jesus over the doorposts of their houses the same way Exodus 12 says the children of Israel did on the first Passover. When they finished, the pastors said, "It doesn't matter that we live here in California where there are earthquakes. The blood of Jesus will protect us from them. It will keep us safe just like the blood of the Passover lamb kept the Israelites while all around them the firstborn in the households of Egypt were all dying."

The next morning, on January 17, at 4:31 a.m., the Northridge earthquake hit the San Fernando Valley. It was a 6.7 magnitude quake which caused estimated damages in excess of $20 billion and caused 57 deaths.

Most of the people who attended our friends' Northridge church found themselves right in the middle of it. Yet by the power of God, they were all supernaturally spared!

Even those who lived in neighborhoods that suffered some of the worst damage came out unharmed. The pastors didn't have any damage to their house except for one broken vase. They had some bookcases with glass doors that moved out into the center of the room, but the glass wasn't broken.

One man who attended the church owned a restaurant. All the other restaurants in the area had to close down because they sustained so much damage. But his came through just fine. He was able to keep it open, and his business increased dramatically because his restaurant was the only one for miles around that was still operating!

One woman of faith who lived in that area owned a house on the side of a hill. The houses on both sides of hers were totally destroyed and had to be condemned. But when the inspectors came out to check her home they found it had stood fast. It was still safe to live in. The structure hadn't sustained any serious damage.

It doesn't matter where you live, you can have the same experience!

If you live in a neighborhood that's full of drugs and violence, you can believe for your home to be a refuge of peace. You can take hold, by faith, of God's supernatural protection, get on your face before Him, and intercede for that place. Stand on those verses in Isaiah 32, believe them and receive them.

Speak Your Faith

In the Name of Jesus, I declare by faith that this is my neighborhood. It's the place where I dwell, and I declare the peace of God over it! I just want to thank You, Lord, that Your angels are camped all around us, according to Psalm 34:7 that says, "The angel of the Lord encamps all around those who fear Him, and delivers them" (NKJV). Your Word, in Psalm 91, says that no evil shall befall us, neither will any plague come near our dwellings (verse 10). Thank You, Lord, that Your peace which transcends all understanding garrisons and mounts guard over our hearts and minds in Christ Jesus (Philippians 4:7, AMPC). Thank You, Lord, for shielding and protecting us!

Jesus said, "Blessed are the peacemakers: for they shall be called the children of God" (Matthew 5:9). So be a peacemaker! Let peace flow through you like a river into your neighborhood, workplace, school and community.

And in the process, you'll be blessed!

Chapter 10

PATIENCE: FAITH'S POWER TWIN

That ye be not slothful, but followers of them who through faith and patience inherit the promises.

HEBREWS 6:12

The fruit of the spirit work in our lives in good times and bad. But it's in the bad times we need them most. It's when others are treating us the worst that we most need the fruit of divine love flowing through us. Or when circumstances look the darkest and problems seem insurmountable, that's when we most need the fruit of joy and peace.

As you've probably discovered from experience, however, it's in the bad times when we're most likely to shut off the flow of those spiritual forces. It's during those times when the trials of life are toughest and seem to drag on and on, that we tend to get weary in well-doing, get out of the spirit and over into the flesh.

That can be a big problem.

How do we solve it?

We yield to the fruit of the spirit that's been given to us by God to help us in those situations. We tap into the powerful force of *patience!*

> Patience is divinely designed to undergird all the other fruit.

It keeps the other fruit of the spirit working so that even when we're under pressure, we don't give up and quit.

Patience is defined in the dictionary as "the quality that does not surrender to circumstances or succumb under trial." It's the opposite of despondency and associated with hope. It speaks of steadfastness of soul under provocation and an attitude of cheerful endurance in the midst of tests and trials.

In the *King James Version* of the Bible, *patience* is translated *longsuffering,* which means "lenience and fortitude."[18] It includes the idea of bearing with ill treatment without giving in to anger or thought of retaliation. Longsuffering is the opposite of hastiness and short temper and describes a person who has the power to exercise revenge but, instead, chooses to exercise restraint.

Longsuffering doesn't just endure difficult people and situations; it does so with a sweet attitude because it's founded on love. And as 1 Corinthians 13 says, "Love endures long and is patient and kind.... Love bears up under anything and everything that comes" (verses 4, 7, AMPC).

When you're facing persecution from other people, patience will help you say, "I am going to walk in love, regardless of what anyone does to me. I'm going to be kind and stay out of strife, no matter what!"

Lack of patience, on the other hand, will push you in the opposite direction. It will cause you to get stressed out over the ugly things people are doing and saying, and all the things that are going wrong. It will

---

18 *Fortitude* is "the mental and emotional strength to face difficulties with courage."

shorten your fuse and make you think, *I've had it with this! I've taken all I'm going to take!*

You have to watch out when you catch yourself giving in to that attitude. You're about to get over on the devil's territory and do something you shouldn't. You're about to break the commandment of love, run out of faith and joy, and exchange victory for defeat.

In most cases, you won't be able to avoid that defeat by just sending up an emergency prayer at the last possible moment, either. You won't be able to transform your attitude instantly by waiting until just before you're about to blow your stack and praying, "God, give me more patience, and give it to me right now!"

Although praying is always a good idea, God can't do very much with that kind of prayer. He can't give us more patience because He's already given us all we'll ever need. He put it inside us when we were born again. Like all the other spiritual fruit—the fruit of the re-created human spirit—it's a part of our new nature. We just need to develop it.

Fruit is much more potent after it's been developed. I found that out when I was a little girl growing up in Arkansas peach country. When the summer days started getting hot, and I went out to find peaches, I learned quickly not to pick the ones that had just appeared on the tree. They hadn't fully developed yet, so they were still mostly seed. They were peaches, but they were small, green, hard and unfit to eat yet. They had to be left on the tree and cultivated until they could fulfill their purpose.

That's how it is with patience. When we receive Jesus as Savior and Lord, it's present within us, but it's like a green peach—it's mostly in seed form. For patience to fulfill its purpose, it has to develop to the point where we can partake of it. It has to be cultivated and watered with the Word.

Pray in Tongues and Practice, Practice, Practice!

Although cultivating patience might not sound very exciting to some people, I like studying and meditating on what the Word says about it because it strengthens me in that area. It heightens my awareness of the supernatural force of patience that's within me. It helps me remember to yield to it so that when I get provoked by something or someone, instead of allowing myself to become short-tempered, I think, *I need to put patience to work in this situation. I need to let my spirit man dominate me right now.*

When contrary people and situations start to wear on you, remembering to yield to patience can make a crucial difference! It can keep you from spouting off in anger or frustration and letting loose with ugly words. It can empower you to hold your tongue when you're about to say things you'll regret.

That's a big deal because once words have been spoken you can't get them back. You can apologize for them, but they'll still be out there in the minds of the people who heard them, and they can continue to cause damage.

Patience can prevent that damage from ever taking place! It can save your marriage. It can save your friendships. It can prevent you from becoming exasperated at work and reacting in a way that may cost you your job.

God will always help you out, of course. He'll even give you some extra grace when you find yourself in a crisis and your patience isn't yet developed enough to handle it.

If you do happen to get into a mess by being impatient, God will always be merciful and help you get back on track.

But the best thing is to not wait to think about patience until you're in a crisis situation. Instead, continually develop it, little by little, day by day.

How do you do that?

One thing you can do is to pray in other tongues. In addition to spending time in the Word and praying with your understanding, praying in tongues helps develop patience because as 1 Corinthians 14:4 says, "He that speaketh in an unknown tongue edifieth himself." When you edify yourself, you're strengthened on the inside. Your inner man is built up. You're able to more easily yield to patience because your spirit gets into the place of dominion where it belongs. It takes charge and begins to rule your mind, will and emotions.

Another way you can develop your patience is by putting it into practice in the small events of everyday life. Take advantage of every opportunity. When you're in the slowest line at the grocery store, rather than getting irritated at the cashier and the people ahead of you, allow patience to come to your aid. Pray God's blessings over everyone around you while you're waiting. When you're stuck in traffic, instead of getting upset, use the extra time in your car to rejoice and praise Jesus for all the wonderful things He's done in your life.

"Well, that sounds good in theory," you might say. "But those kinds of situations are annoying! Practicing patience in them is easier said than done."

Yes, but you *can* do it. You have the patience it takes right there inside you. The only question is: Are you going to use your will to yield to it?

Your will is the gateway to your spirit. Whatever your will decides, that's the way things are going to be. You can use your will either to shut off the outflow of patience within you, or to release it and let it have its perfect work. The choice is up to you.

The consequences, however, are not. Choosing to shut off the force of patience is always costly. Choosing to yield to it will always pay. And in situations in which you are having to use your faith to bring you out of a test or trial, the payoff will be big. It will be big enough to not only get you through whatever trial you're facing, but it will bring you out of it in better shape than you were before it began. Just stay in faith on the Word of God, and patience will help you. It will undergird your faith and bring you out of any test and trial. That's why you can consider it all joy.

This is why the Bible tells us we should actually rejoice when we encounter situations that put a demand on our patience. It's why the New Testament says:

> Consider it wholly joyful, my brethren, whenever you are enveloped in or encounter trials of any sort or fall into various temptations. Be assured and understand that the trial and proving of your faith bring out endurance and steadfastness and patience. But let endurance and steadfastness and patience have full play and do a thorough work, so that you may be [people] perfectly and fully developed [with no defects], lacking in nothing (James 1:2-4, AMPC).

> We glory in tribulations also: knowing that tribulation worketh patience; and patience, experience; and experience, hope: And hope maketh not ashamed... (Romans 5:3-5).

> Blessed (happy, to be envied) is the man who is patient under trial and stands up under temptation, for when he has stood the test and been approved, he will receive [the victor's] crown of life which God has promised to those who love Him (James 1:12, AMPC).

As you can see, patience pays great dividends! So, when you're in a time of trial, don't feel sorry for yourself. Mediate on these scriptures and change your thinking. Make up your mind you are going to consider it all joy, and see that trial as one more opportunity to prove that the Word of God is true. Make up your mind you're going to stay in faith!

Speak Your Faith

I choose to be patient and stay in faith. When this trial is over, I'm going to have that victor's crown! I'm going to be stronger. I'm going to be better. I'm going to have what I believed God for, and be lacking nothing, because I'm not going to quit. I'm going to let patience have her perfect work!

A Lot of Faith, But Not Much Fight

Patience will not only turn trials into triumphs, it will also help you get answers to your prayers. It will help you stay in faith long enough to receive what you've asked for from God. *Staying* in faith is where many believers mess up. They start out well. As Mark 11:24 says, they believe they receive what they ask for when they pray. But when they don't see instant results, they get impatient and start wondering, *Why hasn't the Lord healed me yet? Why hasn't He supplied that need I prayed about?*

Wondering leads to wavering. Wavering makes us like waves being tossed around by the wind. We'll go back and forth between believing and doubting. We'll become double-minded and unstable in our faith.[19]

We can't get anywhere spiritually when we're in that condition!

If you want to receive anything supernatural from the Lord, your faith must stay steady from the moment you pray to the moment the answer manifests. That's the most crucial time in your faith life! It's the

---

19 James 1:6-8: "But let him ask in faith, nothing wavering. For he that wavereth is like a wave of the sea driven with the wind and tossed. For let not that man think that he shall receive any thing of the Lord. A double minded man is unstable in all his ways."

time when things are being set in motion in the spirit realm and yet, in the natural, everything still looks the same. It's the time you're most tempted to get discouraged and say, "Nothing is happening! I've been believing for this for a long time now, and it hasn't come. I give up."

Patience is the force that gives you the strength to overcome that temptation. It enables you to wait in faith without wavering because it never gives up. It keeps believing God without considering symptoms or the passage of time. It will stand and stand, and stand some more, until the manifestation of what was prayed for becomes a reality.

Patience is often the key to receiving a miracle. You don't generally get miracles by just having faith for a few minutes and then caving in. You may have to stand steadfast over time in the face of seeming impossibilities. You have to "fight the good fight of faith" (1 Timothy 6:12).

If you want to see the supernatural happen in your life, you can't be like the man who described himself as having "a lot of faith, but not much fight." You need faith that's aggressive—faith that teams up with patience to pack a one-two punch that puts the devil on the run and brings the impossible to pass!

Ken and I have availed ourselves of that one-two punch time and again over the years. It's what got us through the worst financial trial this ministry ever faced. I'll never forget that trial! It began not long after we launched our daily television broadcast, and it took us almost $6 million into the red. We got so far behind on our television bills that, in the natural, the only way we could ever catch up would be to sell everything we had. Even then, we'd just come out even. The TV bill would be paid but we'd have nothing left.

It was a serious situation, and we needed a supernatural solution!

What did we do?

We went to God's Word that says He supplies all our needs according to His riches in glory by Christ Jesus (Philippians 4:19). We prayed, believed we received and took our stand of faith.

Still, the problem persisted. I can't remember how long it dragged on, but it was a lot longer than we wanted it to be, I can tell you that! We were tempted to get discouraged just like anyone else would, but we kept yielding to patience and overcoming that temptation. We kept God's Word in front of our eyes, in our ears and in our mouths. We stood on what He said and refused to cave in.

Sure enough, over a period of months, the backlog of unpaid TV bills began to dwindle. Then one day, it was completely gone! It didn't disappear all at once. We didn't suddenly get a great deal of money in one lump sum. The money we needed just came in a little at a time, in one way and then another, until we realized we'd experienced a $6 million miracle.

What's more, since we received that miracle, we've never again been in that kind of situation. Why? Because we got stronger during that trial. The Word became bigger in us, patience did its perfect work, and we came out with more faith than ever.

That's just one example, of course. I'm not saying you'll always have to wait months for the answer to your prayer of faith to manifest. Sometimes answers manifest faster, in a matter of hours or days. Other times (as Ken and I can testify) it takes years, and even decades to see what you're believing for come to pass.

The Scriptures are clear about this. Different situations can take different amounts of time. In the Old Testament, when Daniel prayed about a certain matter, he had to wait three weeks to get his answer. The angel who appeared to Daniel explained the delay, indicating to him that in the spirit realm, things had been in motion the whole time. The angel said, "From the first day...thy words were heard, and I am come for thy words.

But the prince of the kingdom of Persia withstood me one and twenty days" (Daniel 10:12-13).

In the New Testament, Jesus had to wait 24 hours to see visible results when He spoke to the fig tree. Even though He operated in perfect faith, after He commanded the fig tree to die, it initially appeared unchanged. The next day, however, when He and His disciples passed by the tree again, it was completely withered up. The change that had begun instantaneously in the unseen realm had manifested, and the tree "dried up from the roots" (Mark 11:20).

That's the way the Spirit of God almost always works in our lives when we're believing for Him to resolve situations. Sometimes He will instantly remove outward physical symptoms, but more often He goes to the root of the problem, and works first in the spirit realm.

While God is working, stand steadfastly in faith until what He is doing in the invisible realm becomes visible.

We have to keep our hearts and our words in agreement with His Word until the problem He's working on withers up like the fig tree and dies. If the process takes an extended period of time, we must keep our patience active and focused on God's Word. Praying in tongues will help build up our spirits, so that while we're waiting, we can obey the command Jesus gave us in Luke.

In your patience possess ye your souls (Luke 21:19).

The Power Twins Will Get the Job Done

Ken calls faith and patience *the power twins.* When you get them working together, they always get the job done. They enable you to "...show the same diligence to the full assurance of hope until the end, that you do not become sluggish, but imitate those who through faith and patience inherit the promises" (Hebrews 6:11-12, NKJV).

Verses 13-15 (NKJV) continue:

> For when God made a promise to Abraham, because He could swear by no one greater, He swore by Himself, saying, "Surely blessing I will bless you, and multiplying I will multiply you." And so, after he had patiently endured, he obtained the promise.

Notice, according to those verses, patience produces diligence. It prevents you from getting spiritually lazy and keeps you doing what you know to do even in those times when your flesh wants to quit. It keeps you acting on and speaking the Word so that when the devil is saying to you, "You're not going to get what you're believing for. You're going to die. You're going to go bankrupt, (or whatever it is), rebuke him! Don't listen! Instead, pay attention to what God says about the situation. **God is always right!**

Speak Your Faith

No, Devil! I have believed that I have received. Therefore, I'm going to have what God said. Even though it hasn't manifested yet in the natural, I say it's mine. I have it now! I rejoice in You, Lord, that Your Word is true. I have the victory, in the Name of Jesus!

When you talk like that, you're following the example of Abram who called himself the "father of many nations" after God changed his name to Abraham when he was a 99-year-old man, and his wife a 90-year-old, barren woman (Genesis 17:4-5; Romans 4:17-18). He confessed his faith in what God had said, and called things that are not as though they were, even after he'd been waiting 25 years for the son God had promised him.

> And being not weak in faith, he considered not his own body now dead, when he was about an hundred years old, neither yet the deadness of Sarah's womb: He staggered not at the promise of God through unbelief; but was strong in faith, giving glory to God; and being fully persuaded that, what he had promised, he was able also to perform (Romans 4:19-21).

Patience had to help Abraham in that situation! It had to come alongside his faith so that in addition to *becoming* fully persuaded he could *remain* fully persuaded, year after year, while he was waiting for that promise to be fulfilled.

On our *Believer's Voice of Victory* television broadcast some years ago, we showed an interview with a family that revealed just how crucial remaining fully persuaded can be. Their son had been in an accident that had severed his spinal cord. His neck had been broken in four places and his ear was cut off. He died six times on the operating table and, though they were able to revive him, he went into a coma.

The doctors said he'd never regain consciousness, and if he survived, he'd be in a permanent vegetative state. But the family chose to stand on God's Word for the boy's healing. They prayed and agreed that he would live and not die and declare the works of the Lord.

For 28 days, they continued to believe and declare the Word over him. For 28 days, even though it looked like nothing was happening, they put faith and patience to work. On day 29, the boy's spinal cord was miraculously put back together. He came out of the coma and kept getting better, until he was totally healed and restored. We showed a video of him running a marathon!

What would have happened if after the first couple of weeks that family had gotten discouraged? What if they'd said, "Maybe the doctors are right, and he'll never be conscious again. Maybe we should quit believing he's going to recover"? That would have been a logical response from a medical standpoint. After seeing that boy lying there day after day in such awful condition, they had every reason in the natural to decide the situation was hopeless and give up.

What if the family had done that? What if they'd quit believing God on day 10 or day 23? What would have happened?

Nothing. That boy would have stayed in the coma and never recovered. That family wouldn't have gotten their miracle because when faith quits, the miraculous quits.

But, praise God, that's not how this situation turned out! This family exercised both faith and patience. They had the Word in their hearts, and the devil couldn't talk them out of it. Impossible circumstances couldn't talk them out of it. They banded together with friends who believed God and stood fast until this family's miracle came.

"But that was a unique situation," someone might say. "We can't always count on getting that kind of miracle."

Oh, yes, we can, if we keep the Word of God planted in our hearts. Jesus assured us of it. He said in the parable of the sower that if we receive the Word and refuse to let it go when trials come against us, if we keep putting the Word first place and don't let other things crowd it out of our hearts, it will always produce results in our lives. It will spring up like the seed that fell on the good ground, and we'll be like "those who, having heard the word with a noble and good heart, keep it and bear fruit *with patience*" (Luke 8:15, NKJV).

Patience, Ministry and Supernatural Power

"But Gloria, you don't understand the kinds of trials I'm going through. You don't know how hard it is to yield to patience in the face of everything and everyone I have to put up with!"

That's true. I don't know everything that's going on with you. But I'm pretty sure of this: It's not any worse than the things the Apostle Paul endured. Compared to him, you and I don't have any trouble. He faced persecution beyond anything most of us today can imagine. Yet he and his fellow ministers remained so steadfast in the Lord that he could give this testimony:

> We give no offense in anything, that our ministry may not be blamed. But in all things we commend ourselves as ministers of God: in much patience, in tribulations, in needs, in distresses, in stripes, in imprisonments, in tumults, in labors, in sleeplessness, in fastings; by purity, by knowledge, by longsuffering, by kindness, by the Holy Spirit, by sincere love... (2 Corinthians 6:3-7, NKJV).

Note that patience and longsuffering are listed in those verses as qualities that attest to someone being a minister of God. They're even connected with the supernatural operations of the Holy Spirit. "Truly the signs of an apostle were wrought," Paul said, "...*in all patience*, in signs, and wonders, and mighty deeds" (2 Corinthians 12:12).

Clearly, if we as ministers want to do anything for God, we have to let patience flow out of us! Second Timothy 4:2 says, "Preach the word; be prepared in season and out of season; correct, rebuke and encourage—with great patience and careful instruction" (NIV).

Why does preaching the Word take patience? Because to get it into people's hearts, we have to preach the same thing over and over. We have to have the attitude Kenneth E. Hagin had. He preached on faith for more than 50 years. One time, someone asked him when was he going to move on and preach about something else? "When you finally get it!" he replied.

Kenneth Hagin knew, even if others didn't, that believers can't get a working revelation of the principles of God's Word by hearing them preached just one time. They have to hear the same messages over and over. They have to keep hearing and hearing the Word of God because it fuels their faith and inspires them to keep acting on what they've heard.

The Day I Jumped Over the Couch

Actually, whether we're the ones preaching or the ones listening, we want to exercise patience when it comes to the Word of God. We want to diligently stick with it, through thick and thin, because the fruit it produces in us (or the lack of it) can make or break us in many different areas of life.

In our relationships with our children, for example, patience can make all the difference in our dealings with them. It can keep us walking in the love of God with them even when they're misbehaving. It can keep us from getting short-tempered and treating them too harshly.

Patience won't make you a pushover. But it will help you keep your emotions in check, so you don't overreact out of frustration. It will help you stay calm, so you can discipline your children in love and help them learn to behave.

I realized very quickly when our son, John, was little that I'd have to draw on the force of divine patience to be a good parent to him. Although I naturally have a calm, steady personality, he really knew how to push my buttons. I rarely lost my temper with him, but a few times he pushed me past my limit!

I remember one time, in particular, when he was about 5 years old, he had spent the whole day aggravating me in one way or another until, in the natural, my patience just ran out. I didn't know much back then about yielding to the fruit of the spirit in pressurized situations. So, without even thinking, I reacted in the flesh.

I can still picture how the scene unfolded. John was on one side of our little family room, and I was on the other. There was a love seat between us and I jumped flat-footed over it and grabbed him! I didn't hurt him, of course, but I sure let him know how angry I was. I left no doubt about the fact that he had pushed me too far!

Even at that early stage in my Christian life, that was an unusual thing for me to do, and I haven't jumped over the couch since. But I did it that day, and even now, almost 50 years later, John still remembers it. He doesn't have many clear recollections of all the times I kept my patience with him. But he has a very clear mental image of me jumping over the couch!

That's typically the way it is. Your kids tend to remember those times you lose your patience. Don't yell at them and get mad. Even when they aggravate you beyond your natural limits, remember to respond to them patiently with the love of God.

When you're dealing with your children, be sure you keep yielding to the supernatural forces of the spirit.

Don't just do that with your children. Make it a point to respond to everyone with the love of God. As Ephesians 4:1-3 says, "...lead a life worthy of your calling.... Always be humble and gentle. Be patient...making allowance for each other's faults because of your love" (NLT).

Just obeying that one command, *making allowances for each other's faults,* would make all of our relationships a lot sweeter! It would solve most of the problems believers have in their marriages. There's no such thing as a perfect husband. There's no such thing as a perfect wife. But we can still have a wonderful time together if we'll choose to love each other anyway and overlook one another's little eccentricities.

I don't know how it is with you and your spouse, but when Ken and I married, we were total opposites. He had to put up with things in me that went against his grain, and I had to put up with things in him that went against mine. Ken has always been very outgoing, for example, but I had always been very quiet. So initially, we had to make allowances for our personality differences in those areas.

Throughout the years, though, we've kind of rubbed off on one another. His influence on me has made me more outgoing. My influence on him has made him a little quieter. As a result, we've both improved. We've modified each other in a very good way.

That's how it's supposed to be in the Church, as well. We're to influence each other for the better. Rather than letting our differences separate us from each other, we're to bear with one another in patience and keep listening to each other so we can all improve and come into unity in the Spirit of **God, who is Love.**

A Beautiful Life

As believers, we're even supposed to let patience flow out of us to the troubled people of this lost world. We're called to reveal the character of Jesus to those who don't know Him by bearing long with them and making allowances for their faults.

When unbelievers see us being patient and kind, it catches their attention. It attracts them to us and opens their hearts so they'll want to hear what we have to say about the Lord.

If we shut off the force of patience, on the other hand, and people see us being irritable and unkind, their hearts will be closed toward us. They won't be interested in what we have to say about Jesus or impressed by the power gifts of the Holy Spirit operating through us if our behavior isn't marked by patience and love.

Patience puts Jesus on display! It's one of the most powerful and beautiful aspects of His nature.

As we consistently fellowship with Him by spending time in prayer and in the Word, we'll bear the fruit of His patience almost unconsciously. Others will start to see it in us, most likely even before we do, and be touched by its sweetness. They'll be more receptive to the gospel because, as Philippians 1:11 says, we are "being filled with the fruits of righteousness, which are by Jesus Christ, unto the glory and praise of God."

> Clothe yourselves therefore, as God's own chosen ones (His own picked representatives), [who are] purified and holy and well-beloved [by God Himself, by putting on behavior marked by] tenderhearted pity and mercy, kind feeling, a lowly opinion of yourselves, gentle ways, [and] patience [which is tireless and long-suffering, and has the power to endure whatever comes, with good temper]. Be gentle and forbearing with one another and, if one has a difference (a grievance or complaint) against another, readily pardoning each other; even as the Lord has [freely] forgiven you... (Colossians 3:12-13, AMPC).

Chapter 11

LET YOUR LIGHT SHINE

But the fruit of the Spirit is love, joy, peace, longsuffering,
kindness, goodness, faithfulness, gentleness, self-control.
GALATIANS 5:22-23, NKJV

The next two spiritual fruit in our study, kindness and goodness, are some of the most delightful. They're so closely connected, they're best understood when examined together. Most Bible scholars agree they're interdependent, and one follows the other, but there's been some debate about which comes first.

Some commentaries say that since kindness gets first mention in Galatians 5:22, it comes first in our experience, and goodness follows. Others say the opposite, that goodness comes first, and produces kindness. Personally, after meditating on the Scriptures and pondering both perspectives, I agree with the latter.

I believe goodness is the foundation for kindness because the Bible describes goodness as a state of being. It says that God *is* good. Goodness isn't just something He has, it's who He is. Since we're re-created in His image, goodness is who we are, too.

W.E. Vine says that kindness signifies "not merely goodness as a quality, rather it is goodness in action, goodness expressing itself in deeds...in grace and tenderness and compassion."[20] Therefore, God's goodness within us is what causes us to be kind. It produces kindness as its result.

I realize I've said this about all the fruit of the spirit, but it's just as true in this case: People are in desperate need of kindness in our world today!

I remember a time when people would never say the kinds of ugly things that are now routinely said, even on media. I remember a day when even unbelievers knew better than to outright curse people in authority and speak openly about them in filthy, hateful ways. These days, however, such vile talk is commonplace and widely accepted!

On social media sites, harsh and slanderous words are flung in every direction. Verbal wars rage. Even ordinary people who are just living their lives and doing the best they know how to do are criticized and ridiculed in very public ways.

Clearly now, more than ever, this world needs the softening influence Christians have to offer. People need for us to put the goodness of God that's within us into action. They need for us to be kind.

What exactly does it mean to be kind? In my studies, I found a number of good definitions.

- *Young's Analytical Concordance to the Bible*[21] defines one of the meanings of *kind* as "useful" or "beneficial" (see Ephesians 4:32, AMPC). So when you're being kind, you're being helpful to others. You're being a blessing to them.

20 *Vine's Expository Dictionary of Biblical Words,* Ed. W.E. Vine, Merrill F. Unger, William White, Jr. (Nashville: Thomas Nelson Publishers, 1985) "good, goodly, goodness," *chrēstotēs,* p. 274.
21 Robert Young, *Young's Analytical Concordance to the Bible* (Peabody, Mass.: Hendrickson Publishers) *chrēstos,* p. 564.

- *Wuest* defines it as "a quality that should pervade and penetrate the whole nature, mellowing in it all that is harsh and austere."[22]

- Webster's dictionary says *kindness* is "the state, quality or habit of being kind, sympathetic, friendly, gentle, tender hearted, generous, affectionate, well-dispositioned, and courteous."

- In *Sparkling Gems From the Greek,* Rick Renner says, "Kindness is goodness in action, sweetness of disposition, gentleness in dealing with others, benevolence, kindness, affability. The word describes the ability to act for the welfare of those taxing your patience. The Holy Spirit removes abrasive qualities from the character of one under His control."[23]

- Donald Gee equates kindness with gentleness but says it "must never be confused with mere weakness. Gentleness [or kindness] is power under perfect control."[24]

Do those definitions accurately describe your personality and how you interact with others? They should, because that's who you really are on the inside. As a partaker of God's goodness, you are kind!

You aren't like people in the world. They aren't born again, so they tend to be harsh. So many have sharp-edged personalities because they don't have the Spirit of God dwelling in them. Their inner man hasn't been remade with the light and life of God. As Ephesians 4:18 (NIV) says, "They are darkened in their understanding and separated from the

22 Kenneth S. Wuest, *Wuest's Word Studies: Galatians in the Greek New Testament for the English Reader* (Grand Rapids: Wm. B. Eerdmans Publishing Co., 1966) p. 160.
23 Rick Renner, *Sparkling Gems From the Greek* (Tulsa: Harrison House Publishers, 2003) p. 534.
24 Donald Gee, *The Fruit of the Spirit,* Rev. Edition (Springfield: Gospel Publishing House, 2010) p. 53.

life of God because of the ignorance that is in them due to the hardening of their hearts."

> That, however, is not the way of life you learned when you heard about Christ [Jesus] and were taught in him...to put on the new self, created to be like God in true righteousness and holiness.... Do not let any unwholesome talk come out of your mouths, but only what is helpful for building others up according to their needs, that it may benefit those who listen. And do not grieve the Holy Spirit of God, with whom you were sealed for the day of redemption. Get rid of all bitterness, rage and anger, brawling and slander, along with every form of malice. Be kind and compassionate to one another, forgiving each other, just as in Christ God forgave you (verses 20-21, 24, 29-32, NIV).

Draw Your Words Out of Your New Identity

Notice, according to those verses, one of the primary ways the fruit of kindness manifests is in how you talk to people. Being kind in your communications with others expresses to them the goodness of God that's inside you. Speaking sharp, unedifying words hinders the expression of that goodness because they're not reflective of your new self.

This is something most of us need to be reminded of often so we don't slip into bad habits. We can let the *un*kindness of this world seep into our speech and make us abrasive with people. Or, we can get into the flesh, and sometimes even get so focused on what we're doing in the natural that we might not intend to be unkind, but we inadvertently come across as harsh. As believers, that's not what we want to do. We want to speak gently, to yield to the kindness that's in our hearts when we're interacting with others.

We want to say things in a way that builds people up and encourages them.

No one enjoys being around someone with a sharp tongue, but everyone enjoys being spoken to with courtesy, gentleness and compassion. So, if we'll just hook up our tongues to our new nature, it will do wonders for our social lives! People will be drawn to us. They'll want to hear what we have to say because they're hungry for the fruit of kindness they experience when they're with us.

"But Gloria," someone might say, "I'm just not the soft-spoken type. I've always been brusque and edgy. I guess it was the way I grew up. My dad was sharp-tongued, and I'm just like him."

You're right! You *are* just like your Dad—just not the way you think. You're like your heavenly Father—God. Spiritually, you've been born of Him. In your flesh, you may still have some of the unkind ways of communicating you learned from your earthly father, but you're not in bondage to those ways anymore. They're part of your "old self." When your flesh tries to default to those old brusque habits, refuse to give in to it. Put on your "new self"! Let your new nature of love on the inside show up on the outside, and walk in it.

Speak Your Faith

No! I'm not yielding to harshness. I'll not talk that way anymore. I'll draw my words out of my new identity because it's just like God. My new identity is good and gentle and kind. I open my mouth with wisdom, and in my tongue is the law of kindness (Proverbs 31:26)!

Then, act on that faith confession. Follow the example of Jesus in your communications—talk to people like He and your heavenly Father would. Do what Ephesians 5:1 tells us to do: "Be imitators of God, therefore, as dearly loved children" (NIV-84).

I remember when our grandson Max was a little boy, he liked to imitate Ken. He'd watch the movie *Covenant Rider*, where Ken played the part of a cowboy, and then he'd do what he saw Ken do in the movie. He'd carry around his toy gun and knife and wear his cowboy boots. He'd follow Covenant Rider's example every way he could because he wanted to be just like his *Paw-Paw!*

That's what we're to do where God is concerned. We're to walk in His ways, talk like He talks and wear His nature. We're to put away the old habits and patterns we had before we were born again—patterns of selfishness and hardness toward other people—and replace them with new patterns that are like our heavenly Father's. We're to imitate Him, and He is kind!

Sadly, many people, Christians included, don't realize how kind God actually is. They think of Him as being harsh, quick to judge and criticize. They think if they do something He doesn't like, He'll just cut them off at the knees, so to speak.

The Bible, however, contradicts such ideas. It says:

> I am the Lord, who exercises kindness (Jeremiah 9:24, NIV).

> O praise the Lord, all ye nations: praise him, all ye people. For his merciful kindness is great toward us (Psalm 117:1-2).

> With everlasting kindness will I have mercy on thee, saith the Lord thy Redeemer (Isaiah 54:8).

> The Most High...is kind to the unthankful and evil (Luke 6:35, NKJV).

> [He designed the plan of Redemption so] that in the ages to come he might show the exceeding riches of His grace in His kindness toward us in Christ Jesus (Ephesians 2:7, NKJV).

Kindness attracts people to us and to Jesus who's inside us.

God needs for us to manifest His kindness because it's a witness to the world. When unbelievers see us being tender and benevolent, they realize there's something different about us. When they see us acting like our Father, speaking kind words and doing kind deeds, they start thinking, *I wish I could be like that!* So, they're likely to be interested when we tell them about the Lord.

What's more, when we sow kindness into other people's lives, we reap kindness in our own lives in return. People treat us better and hold us in higher regard. They tend to speak well of us and do nice things for us.

This principle is confirmed repeatedly in the Scriptures:

A kindhearted woman gains respect...[and] a kind man benefits himself, but a cruel man brings trouble on himself (Proverbs 11:16-17, NIV-84).

[The virtuous woman] openeth her mouth with wisdom; and in her tongue is the law of kindness.... Her children arise up, and call her blessed; her husband also, and he praiseth her (Proverbs 31:26, 28).

Do not let kindness and truth leave you; bind them around your neck, write them on the tablet of your heart. So you will find favor and good repute in the sight of God and man (Proverbs 3:3-4, NASB).

Therefore, as God's chosen people, holy and dearly loved, clothe yourselves with...kindness (Colossians 3:12, NIV).

Come to Jesus and Get a Fresh Supply

"Yes, I know those verses are in the Bible," you might say, "but my life is so hectic, I'm too tired to even think about whether or not I'm being kind. I don't have the energy."

I understand. Better yet, so does Jesus. He knows how draining the challenges of life can sometimes be, and He told us in the New Testament how to get recharged. He said:

> Come unto me, all ye that labour and are heavy laden, and I will give you rest. Take my yoke upon you, and learn of me; for I am meek and lowly in heart: and ye shall find rest unto your souls. For my yoke is easy, and my burden is light (Matthew 11:28-30).

So what do we do when we're exhausted and running short on kindness? We run to Jesus! He's the Source of the fruit of the spirit in our lives. He's our Deliverer. He's the One who enables us to be gracious and thoughtful and helpful to others. We don't do it in our own ability. We don't do it by straining and working at it in the natural.

We walk in the fruit of the spirit through our union and fellowship with Him.

"Come to Me," Jesus said. Don't look at the circumstances that have risen up against you. Don't look at the people around you and say, "Well, they never help me. They don't care anything about me." When you're looking to circumstances and people, you're looking in the wrong place.

Look to the Lord! His yoke is *easy*. Or, as that verse can also be translated, His yoke is *kind*.[25] You can always get a fresh supply of kindness from Jesus because He has an abundance of it, and He's eager to minister

---

25 *Vine's Expository Dictionary of Biblical Words*, "easy, easier, easily," *chrēstos*, p. 192.

it to you. He's waiting with open arms, eager to help you, to pour out His mercy on you, and to lift the burdens off your shoulders.

He won't just barge in uninvited, however, and take those burdens away from you. He won't force His rest and refreshing on you. You have to give Him an opening by getting into His Word and His presence. You have to "draw nigh to God, and he will draw nigh to you" (James 4:8).

Don't wait until you're in a desperate situation to draw near to Him, either. Don't just look to Him as your last resort and be like the fellow whose friend asked for prayer and he responded, "Oh, my...has it come to *that?*" Cultivate the habit of praying about everything. Come to Jesus every day.

Spend time with Him in the morning before you see anyone else, and then draw nigh to Him throughout the day. Run to Him the moment you sense you're getting weary.

Live in such continual fellowship with Him that when a problem comes up and you need an answer for it, He's your first thought.

Speak Your Faith

Lord, You're my refuge. You're my high tower. You're my ever-present help in time of trouble—the fountain of living waters. You're the One who restores and refreshes my soul when it runs dry. Your Word says in Isaiah 40:31 that if I wait on You, You will renew my strength and cause me to mount up with wings like an eagle. I believe I receive Your refreshing and renewing and strength today, as only

You can give. I declare that I am strong in You, and in the power of Your might!

Remember, Jesus is there for you, always. He's ready and approachable. He's full of kindness, love, joy and peace, and He'll pour those things into you until your heart overflows. "Therefore come boldly unto the throne of grace...obtain mercy, and find grace to help in time of need" (Hebrews 4:16).

Disposed to Show Favors

Just as Jesus is the Source of kindness, He's also its counterpart: the spiritual fruit of goodness. As I said at the beginning of this chapter, Goodness is who God is. It's His nature, and because He's in us, it's our nature too.

Wuest defines *goodness* as "that quality in a man who is ruled by and aims at what is good, namely the quality of moral worth."[26] Webster's dictionary describes it as "the state of or quality of being good," and says it refers specifically to "virtue, excellence, kindness, generosity and benevolence."

Personally, when I think about goodness, I always think about my granddaddy. He was one of the best people I've ever known. When I was a little girl, he seemed to me to be goodness personified! He could put up with anything and still retain a sweet attitude. In all the years I knew him, I never saw him get angry or lose his temper. No matter what happened, he could bear up under it in an amazingly gracious way.

He was also benevolent and loved to show favor. He was always giving. He'd give to us grandkids anything he had. He'd let us drive his pickup truck into town to go see a movie even before we had driver's licenses.

My granddaddy was so goodhearted, there would have been no limit to what he would have done for us. My grandmother wasn't quite as

---

26 Wuest, *Word Studies From the Greek New Testament*, Vol. 1.

tolerant and giving as he was, so when I wanted to ask for something, I went to him because I was confident he wouldn't turn me down!

That's how we ought to be in our relationship with God. Whenever we need or want something, we should go to Him, fully expecting to receive from Him what we ask. We should be confident He'll give it to us and not turn us down (John 14:13, 15:16, 16:23-24; Matthew 21:21; Luke 12:32; Mark 11:24).

Why? Because He is good...good...good!

All through the Bible, goodness is cited as the most outstanding attribute of God's nature.

That's what God revealed to Moses when Moses asked to see God's glory. God said, "I will cause *all my goodness* to pass in front of you" (Exodus 33:19, NIV). God "passed by before him, and proclaimed, 'The Lord, The Lord God, merciful and gracious, longsuffering, and abundant in goodness and truth'" (Exodus 34:6).

Psalm 145:8-9 describes God in much the same way. It says, "The Lord is gracious, and full of compassion; slow to anger, and of great mercy. The Lord is good to all: and his tender mercies are over all his works."

The word *gracious* means "disposed to show favors." It means God is easily entreated. He wants to show Himself strong in your behalf and do you good. He's so *full* of compassion, there's no room for anything else in Him. His mercy is so vast, the Bible describes it as *great*. His benevolence is so comprehensive, He is good to *all!*

Those are amazing statements, even when applied to God. Yet they should also apply to the Church. We ought to be living so in line with the Scriptures that the world sees in us God's great mercy and benevolence. We ought to be expressing our natural, supernatural disposition to such a degree that unbelievers see us as people who will help and care for them as God cares for them, and not take advantage of them.

The world needs to see us that way because it's the goodness of God that leads sinners to repentance (Romans 2:4), and most sinners don't have any idea how good He is. The devil has so slandered God's good Name that most people think He's behind all the calamities that take place on this earth. They mistakenly think He's causing them problems, making them sick and sending trouble their way. Many people have even been religiously taught that God does those things to punish them or to teach them something.

Yet nothing could be further from the truth!

> The Bible declares from beginning to end that God is good.

God has all power at His disposal, and His greatest desire is to use it all to help people and bless them. He even designed nature to testify to this. As Acts 14:15-17 says:

> ...God, which made heaven, and earth, and the sea, and all things that are therein...suffered all nations to walk in their own ways. Nevertheless he left not himself without witness, in that he did good, and gave us rain from heaven, and fruitful seasons, filling our hearts with food and gladness.

The goodness of God is great news to people who are lost in the darkness of this world! It's like a lifeline that draws them out of the darkness and pulls them toward the light. But sadly, the Church hasn't always offered that lifeline to people. We haven't consistently preached about God's goodness and put it on display.

Kenneth E. Hagin used to say, for example, that in the 1950s when Oral Roberts began preaching the message that *God is a good God,* many ministers actually got mad at him for saying that.

"I wish Oral Roberts would stop saying that!" they told Brother Hagin.

"What do you want him to say? That God is a bad God?" he asked.

"No," they'd reply. "But just saying He's good gives people the wrong impression."

Why did those ministers think that calling God *good* would leave the wrong impression? Because they'd bought into a religious lie. They believed that God sometimes does bad things for reasons we don't understand. They believed God is the One who brought calamity on Job, for instance, and that He is the One who sent Paul a thorn in the flesh.

Those beliefs are still common today in some religious circles, but they're contrary to the Bible. It says the calamities Job experienced and Paul's thorn in the flesh came from Satan. It affirms God's goodness and testifies of it, time and again, in verses like these:

Oh how great is thy goodness, which thou hast laid up for them that fear thee; which thou hast wrought for them that trust in thee before the sons of men! (Psalm 31:19).

Good and upright is the Lord: therefore will he teach sinners in the way (Psalm 25:8).

Oh that men would praise the Lord for his goodness, and for his wonderful works to the children of men! For he satisfieth the longing soul, and filleth the hungry soul with goodness (Psalm 107:8-9).

For thou, Lord, art good, and ready to forgive; and plenteous in mercy unto all them that call upon thee (Psalm 86:5).

God anointed Jesus of Nazareth with the Holy Ghost and with power: who went about doing good, and healing all that were oppressed of the devil; for God was with him (Acts 10:38).

A Good Book for a Good Life

Look again at that last verse. Jesus, who perfectly revealed the Father, went about *doing good*. He went about not only preaching God's goodness, but also demonstrating it in ways everyone could see.

The earthly ministry of Jesus totally shocked the religious people of His day. He showed them a side of God they'd never seen. They'd never been taught much about the goodness of God—much less toward sinners! They'd been told He demanded everything had to be done just a certain way or He would punish and reject them, and they couldn't come around Him anymore.

"Well," someone might say, "that was true, wasn't it? In Old Testament times, didn't God give people a lot of laws and tell them that if they didn't obey Him, something bad would happen?"

Yes, He did give the Old Covenant Law and the commandments, but for a very important purpose. He certainly didn't do it to bind and control people.

God gave His laws and commandments so that His people could be protected from the curse that had already come on the earth through sin. He taught His people His principles and precepts so they could live in a way that would bring them THE BLESSING that was His heart's desire for them. He wanted to do them good! As Moses said, "The Lord commanded us to do all these statutes, to fear the Lord our God, for our good always, that he might preserve us alive, as it is at this day" (Deuteronomy 6:24).

Under the old covenant, however, God's people didn't have born-again spirits, so they didn't have it in their hearts to obey Him. They continually rebelled against Him and went their own way. Yet even then, God still yearned to do them good. He still said:

> O that there were such an heart in them, that they would fear me, and keep all my commandments always, that it might be well with them, and with their children for ever! (Deuteronomy 5:29).

> O that thou hadst hearkened to my commandments! then had thy peace been as a river, and thy righteousness as the waves of the sea (Isaiah 48:18).

That was God's heart for His people under the old covenant. Just think how much He wants to pour out His goodness in the new covenant on His born-again sons and daughters (Hebrews 8:6)! We've been washed by the blood of Jesus and made one spirit with Him. Don't you think He wants us to enjoy a good and blessed life?

Certainly, He does!

That's why He gave us His written Word. This earth can be a dark place because of sin and the devil who's behind it. Bad things are out there. The curse is out there. But if we'll find out what God said in the Scriptures and do it, we can live above the darkness and the curse, and abide in the light. If we'll continue in the Word, we'll be Jesus' disciples, and as He said, "Ye shall know the truth, and the truth shall make you free" (John 8:32).

The Word of God is a freedom Book! It isn't a set of rules or just a list of do's and don'ts.

> *God's Word is a good Book, written by our good God, to show us how to receive and walk in the abundance of His goodness all the days of our lives.*

What does it mean to walk in God's goodness?

It means that we receive His blessings in every area of our lives—spirit, soul, body, financially and socially—and that we share those blessings with others. It means we do what Jesus did when He was on earth: We go about doing good and healing all that are oppressed of the devil (Acts 10:38).

"But Gloria," you might say, "I'm not a minister; I'm just a believer. I can't go around acting like Jesus!"

He said you can. In John 14:12, He said, "He that believeth on me, the works that I do shall he do also; and greater works than these shall he do; because I go unto my Father." And in Mark 16:17-18, He said, "These signs shall follow them that believe; In my name shall they cast out devils; they shall speak with new tongues...they shall lay hands on the sick, and they shall recover."

Every born-again believer ought to be doing what Jesus talked about in those verses. We ought to be ministering the healing power of God to the sick, casting out devils, sharing the Word of God with people, and helping them get delivered!

God is ready and able to do those things through us. He just needs us to stop being so caught up in the natural things of this life and start paying more attention to His leadings. He needs for us to walk with Him day by day, and allow the fruit of the spirit He's put within us to flow out to others.

The more we'll do that, the more we'll see revival in this earth. The more we'll do that, the more people will see God's goodness through us and come running to Him!

Good Trees Bear Good Fruit

It isn't always easy to extend God's goodness to people, of course. Sometimes they'll make it difficult for us. They'll behave in ways that aggravate us, they'll mistreat us, and may be even downright mean to us. When they do, we'll be presented with a choice: Will we get mad and express ill will toward them? Or will we be like our heavenly Father and express "good will toward men" (Luke 2:14)?

To be able to express goodwill toward others, we must align our wills with God's will. We must choose to yield to His goodness within us and allow it to overcome the selfish tendencies of our flesh. We must remember that because we're born of God, and He has goodwill toward men, we can have goodwill toward men, too.

Unsaved people don't have the nature of God within them. They're still living in the kingdom of darkness. So, when they're under pressure, they follow the dictates of their fallen human nature. They automatically go the world's way, walking in selfishness and looking out for themselves.

Jesus said, "Make a tree good and its fruit will be good, or make a tree bad and its fruit will be bad" (Matthew 12:33, NIV). So, don't be surprised and upset when unbelievers bear bad fruit. Realize it's normal for them because they're still joined to the bad tree of sin.

For us as believers, however, bearing bad fruit is not normal at all. We've been grafted into the good tree of God by faith in the Lord Jesus Christ. Because we're in Him and He's in us, we are "full of goodness" (Romans 15:14).

Alexander Maclaren wrote, "A man must first be good in order to do good."[27] Through the new birth, we've been *re-created* good. We have within us everything it takes to do good in every situation, and that's what the Lord has commanded us to do.

---

27   Maclaren, "Galatians: The Fruit of the Spirit," in *Expositions of Holy Scripture.*

He's said to us in scripture after scripture:

Love your enemies, do good to them which hate you (Luke 6:27).

Live as children of light (for the fruit of the light consists in all goodness, righteousness and truth) (Ephesians 5:8-9, NIV).

Be not overcome of evil, but overcome evil with good (Romans 12:21).

As we have therefore opportunity, let us do good unto all men, especially unto them who are of the household of faith (Galatians 6:10).

Live such good lives among the pagans that, though they accuse you of doing wrong, they may see your good deeds and glorify God on the day he visits us (1 Peter 2:12, NIV).

Let your light shine before men, that they may see your good deeds and praise your Father in heaven (Matthew 5:16, NIV-84).

Be careful to maintain good works. These things are good and profitable unto men (Titus 3:8).

Walk worthy of the Lord unto all pleasing, being fruitful in every good work (Colossians 1:10).

For we are his workmanship, created in Christ Jesus unto good works, which God hath before ordained that we should walk in them (Ephesians 2:10).

Therefore to him that knoweth to do good, and doeth it not, to him it is sin (James 4:17).

For it is God which worketh in you both to will and to do of his good pleasure (Philippians 2:13).

I quote that last scripture a lot. I make it my confession of faith, especially at those times when I'm not be feeling very enthusiastic about the good things I'm called to do. When it's cold outside, for instance, and I don't really want to get all my books together and go to the TV studio to tape broadcasts for *Believer's Voice of Victory,* I often thank the Lord for Philippians 2:13!

Speak Your Faith

Lord, I thank You that You energize and create in me the power and desire to will and to work for Your good pleasure, satisfaction and delight (Philippians 2:13, AMPC). Thank You that I don't have to do anything in my own strength. I can do the things I am required to do today in Your strength by depending on You. I am empowered to do good wherever I go, by the life of God that's within me. I am happy to do the good things God has called me to do! I can do all things through the Anointed One and His Anointing, which strengthens me (Philippians 4:13)!

I remind myself that I'm empowered to do good by the life of God that's within me. God's burden-removing, yoke-destroying power within me makes good works a joy and not a burden. It stirs up my faith so that I'm happy to do the good things God has called me to do.

This is yet another benefit of looking to the Spirit of God within us each day and walking in fellowship with Him. We don't have to mentally decide to manifest God's goodness each time the opportunity arises. It becomes our natural response, our normal way of life.

When the devil assaults our minds with bad thoughts and temptations, we automatically drive them out with good thoughts and confessions from God's Word. Goodness becomes our lifestyle, and we become known for it. We acquire a reputation for being and doing good.

That's the way it was with certain people in the early Church, like Dorcas, for example, in Acts 9. She was known for her goodness and was a wonderful testimony to the Lord Jesus Christ because she was "full of good works and almsdeeds which she did" (verse 36). The same was true of Barnabas. Acts 11:24 says, "He was a good man, and full of the Holy Ghost and of faith."

Those are the kinds of things people should be able to say about you and me. They should be able to say, "She's a good woman." Or, "He's a good man." That's the highest label anyone could put on your life. There's not anything anyone could say about you that could be better.

I heard a story one time about a young man who'd had a very hard childhood. He'd grown up in a rough neighborhood, surrounded by abuse and ungodliness. His mother had been killed in an accident, and she was the family's only connection to God.

After his mother died, the young man turned to drugs. He used them, sold them and spent some time in prison. When he got out of prison, he wanted to change his life, so he went looking for help. Figuring God was his only hope, he asked the local drug dealer, in whose house he happened to be staying at the time, if he knew of a good church.

"I don't know of a good church," the drug dealer answered, "but I know a good woman."

Think about a drug dealer making that statement! Think about what that woman must have been like to have made such an impression on him. She must have been so loving and so faithful to pray and do good that everyone in the neighborhood had heard of her. Not just the Christians but even the local drug dealer knew her reputation for doing good.

The troubled young man got in touch with this woman, and she shared the gospel with him. She took him to her church where he made Jesus the Lord of his life, became a new creature in Christ and was delivered from drugs. After a while, his father followed in his footsteps, telling his son: "I watched you, and thought if you could do it, I could do it."

See how that worked? One good woman became a testimony to the goodness of God and drew one young man to Jesus. He became a testimony to God's goodness and drew his father to the Lord.

God's goodness manifested through you changes others! It's a light to those around you that makes them want what you have. So, yield to that supernatural force of goodness within you. Put it on display for all to see.

Let your light shine!

Chapter 12

FAITHFULNESS PAYS

*Most men will proclaim every one his own
goodness: but a faithful man who can find?*

PROVERBS 20:6

Normally, there's nothing particularly fascinating about watching someone working in a flower bed. But some years ago, I saw a fellow doing that in a way I'll never forget. What first caught my attention about him was how little actual work he was doing. He'd apparently been hired to break up the ground and chop the weeds out of the flower bed, but he didn't seem at all committed to getting the job done.

He'd work for a few minutes, then he'd stop and just stand there with his hand on his hip, doing nothing. After a while, he'd halfheartedly poke around at the weeds a little more. Then he'd take another break and stand there looking around again.

He obviously wasn't doing something he wanted to do. Perhaps he didn't think hoeing weeds was much fun or he didn't consider it very important. As I watched him, it occurred to me that even though cleaning out a flower bed might not be thrilling work, he'd clearly accepted the task and was getting paid to do it. So, the honorable thing would have been for him to give it his best effort and to do the finest job he possibly could.

It's not honorable when you're getting paid by the hour, to spend part of that hour goofing off. It's not right to take a job and then treat it like it doesn't matter. Yet such behavior is commonplace in this world.

It's even common among Christians!

Why? Because so many Christians haven't developed one very important fruit of the spirit in their lives. They haven't developed the fruit of faithfulness.

Translated from the Greek word *pistis*, the word *faithfulness* means "steadfastness," "trustworthiness" and "consistency." It's defined in Webster's dictionary as "firmly adhering to duty; true fidelity; loyal, true to allegiance; constant in the performance of duties or services."

Bible scholar Kenneth Wuest defines *faithfulness* as being "fidelity as produced in the life of the yielded Christian by the Holy Spirit."[28] Alexander Maclaren describes it as a quality that's to be evident in the life of every believer—not only where spiritual endeavors are concerned but in natural affairs as well—and says, "The Christian life is to manifest itself in the faithful discharge of all duties and the honest handling of all things committed to it."[29]

Faithfulness causes you to be dependable, true to your word and diligent to fulfill the responsibilities you've been given.

Faithfulness causes you to put forth persistent effort to accomplish whatever you've committed to undertake. When you have the force of faithfulness flowing in your life, you can be trusted to do what's right

28 Wuest, *Wuest's Word Studies From the Greek New Testament*, 160.
29 Maclaren, "Galatians: The Fruit of the Spirit," in *Expositions of Holy Scripture.*

even when no one is looking. Your employer doesn't have to watch over you every minute to make sure you're not goofing off. He doesn't have to wonder if you're going to do your work for the day. He knows he can count on you to attend to his business as if it were your own.

In the world, faithfulness is scarce. It's a rare commodity. But as believers, we should be famous for being faithful! We should be known by everyone, everywhere, for being the most dependable and trustworthy people anyone has ever seen, because we have an endless supply of faithfulness available to us. We've inherited the faithfulness of our heavenly Father.

Talk about Someone who's famous for faithfulness! Time and again, the Bible says about Him:

> Thy faithfulness reacheth unto the clouds (Psalm 36:5).
>
> Thy faithfulness is unto all generations (Psalm 119:90).
>
> O Lord God Almighty! Where is there anyone as mighty as you, Lord? Faithfulness is your very character (Psalm 89:8, NLT-96).
>
> God is faithful, by whom ye were called unto the fellowship of his Son Jesus Christ our Lord (1 Corinthians 1:9).
>
> The Lord is faithful, who shall stablish you, and keep you from evil (2 Thessalonians 3:3).
>
> If we believe not, yet he abideth faithful: he cannot deny himself (2 Timothy 2:13).

Look again at that last verse. It identifies faithfulness as an inseparable part of God Himself. It's a fundamental aspect of His identity that makes Him who He is. God's heart of integrity, truthfulness and faithfulness so defines Him that to be unfaithful, God would have to deny Himself!

The devil, of course, doesn't want people to know this. So over the years, he's promoted religious doctrines that refute it. He's tried to undermine our confidence in God by telling us we can't always count on Him to keep His promises to us, or that He won't always be faithful to fulfill His Word. "You just never know what God's going to do," Satan says. "He might come through in the lives of some people now and then, but you can't always depend on Him to come through for *you.*"

Those statements are false! According to the Scriptures, God is "reliable, trustworthy, and therefore ever true to His promise, and He can be depended on" (1 Corinthians 1:9, AMPC). He's so unchangeable that even if "we...[do not believe and are untrue to Him], He remains true (faithful to His Word and His righteous character)" (2 Timothy 2:13, AMPC).

Because of His great love for His people, we see in the Old Testament that God was faithful in His dealings with the often-unfaithful Israelites! He gave them His commandments and essentially told them if they obeyed Him, they would be blessed. The curse that came on the earth because of Adam's sin would not be able to come on them (Deuteronomy 28:1-15).

God wanted with all His heart for the Israelites to obey Him. He so loved them and wanted things to go well with them. That's why He told them how to live and walk in His ways. But when they rebelled against Him, and did things that opened the door to the curse, He didn't interfere. He remained faithful to His Word, and what He'd said came to pass. The curse that was in the earth because of sin *did* come upon them. Even though it grieved His loving heart, He had already told them how it would be, and it happened just as He said it would.

Today, God is still the same as He's always been. Though we are living under a new covenant, God is still faithful to His Word. If He says to us in the Scriptures that something won't work, and we choose to do it anyway, just as with the Old Covenant Israelites, our lives aren't going to work in that area. If He tells us certain behaviors and attitudes will bring a certain result, that's the way it's going to be.

God won't change His Word and His ways to accommodate us because He said in Malachi 3:6, "I am the Lord, I change not." And Hebrews 13:8 says Jesus is the same yesterday, today and forever. If someone is going to change, it will have to be us!

Called, Chosen and Faithful

We do have it better than the Israelites did, though. Under the new covenant, we can immediately repent and receive forgiveness (1 John 1:9). We can go boldly to God's throne, obtain mercy and grace, and continue to be blessed (Hebrews 4:16).

Why? Because of the faithfulness of Jesus!

Jesus came to Earth more than 2,000 years ago and bore the curse for us. He took upon Himself flesh and "was faithful to him that appointed him" (Hebrews 3:2). Jesus carried out God's plan so that we could be redeemed. He overcame temptation on our behalf and defeated the devil at every turn. Jesus walked in such total victory and authority every moment of His earthly life that no matter what Satan did, he could find no place in Him (John 14:30).

The ultimate example of faithfulness, Jesus went to the cross and laid down His life to pay the price for our sins! In the Garden of Gethsemane, He sweat blood over the prospect of being separated from His Father and subjected Himself to Satan's dominion for three days and nights. But Jesus remained faithful to His mission. He endured the Cross, was raised from the dead and ascended into heaven "that he might be a merciful and *faithful* high priest...to make reconciliation for the sins of the people" (Hebrews 2:17).

Just think about the absolute faithfulness of Jesus! He was faithful to go to the Cross and shed His blood to wipe out the sins of our past when we are born again. And even now, when we sin, we have His promise in 1 John 1:9 that says, "If we confess our sins, he is *faithful* and just to forgive us our sins, and to cleanse us from all unrighteousness."

Jesus' own faithfulness resides in our born-again spirits!

Jesus is as faithful today as He's ever been. He lives inside us by His Spirit. That means we have the same capacity to be faithful that He has. We can be faithful, even when circumstances are challenging and when finishing our race on this earth seems hard.

That's why God can tell us in Revelation 2:10 to "remain faithful even when facing death" (NLT). We have the ability to do it! We have Jesus, "the faithful and true witness" dwelling inside us (Revelation 3:14). He has declared that we are "called, and chosen, and faithful" (Revelation 17:14) and what He declares about us is the truth!

"But Gloria, I'm just not naturally a very dependable person," you might say. "I have a track record of acting unfaithfully in a lot of different ways."

I don't care what your natural track record is. If you're a believer, you should be agreeing with what Jesus says about you. Repent of your past mistakes, trust Jesus as your faithful High Priest to forgive and cleanse you, and then start saying what He says about you.

Speak Your Faith

According to God's Word in Revelation 17:14, I am faith-ful. I have the force of faithfulness within me because Jesus, the faithful One, dwells in me. I choose to yield to His faithfulness in me. So I declare that I walk in the fruit of faithfulness. I am faithful in every area of my life, and I will continue to be faithful to what God has called me to do all the days of my life!

As a believer, you can say such things with boldness because your faithfulness isn't dependent on your own natural strength and abilities. Your faithfulness is founded on the supreme fact that *God* is faithful. He's faithful to watch over His Word to perform it, and He has said in His Word that you are faithful. Therefore, as you believe and confess that, the Holy Spirit goes to work to bring it to pass in your life.

Donald Gee, in his book on the fruit of the spirit, gave a wonderful illustration of this principle he heard from his friend, Pentecostal pioneer Howard Carter, "likening our human natures in all their unreliability to the loose powder of cement. But when water is mixed with the cement it turns into concrete hard as a rock. So the living water of God's Holy Spirit can turn our lack of steadfastness into magnificent faithfulness, and convert many an impulsive 'Simon' into a devoted 'Peter.'"[30]

Faithfulness is a force you want working in your life—especially if you want God to pour out His power and blessing through you.

Faithfulness is a wonderful thing! As 2 Chronicles 16:9 says, "The eyes of the Lord run to and fro throughout the whole earth, to show Himself strong on behalf of those whose heart is loyal [or faithful] to Him" (NKJV). And, 1 Corinthians 4:2 says, "It is required in stewards that one be found faithful" (NKJV).

God is searching all the time for people He can trust who will follow through when He gives them an assignment. He's looking for faithful

---

30   Gee, *The Fruit of the Spirit,* p. 48.

men and women who will get the job done at any cost, regardless of inconvenience or discomfort. God can show Himself strong through those people because they can be trusted to do what's right. He can entrust to them His power and riches. And He can continually increase them because they can always be counted on to be faithful to do with His resources what He tells them to do.

Others can count on faithful people too, because faithfulness to God necessitates faithfulness to men. When we're faithful to both, it puts us at a tremendous advantage. It causes us to be favored and promoted not only spiritually but naturally, as well.

When a Lion Becomes Your Pillow

Faithfulness pays!

If you'll develop and grow strong in it, it will come to your rescue in many different ways. It will cause your life to work and make you a success—spiritually and naturally. It will increase your income and influence. Proverbs says, "A faithful man shall abound with blessings" (28:20), "The hand of the diligent maketh rich" (10:4) and, "The hand of the diligent shall bear rule: but the slothful shall be under tribute" (12:24). You can see diligence and faithfulness at work in the life of Joseph in the Old Testament. In Genesis 39, Joseph was sold as a slave to Potiphar, who was an Egyptian officer in Pharaoh's army. Even though Joseph was in a difficult situation, he set his heart to be diligent in serving his master, the Egyptian.

Verse 4 says, "And Joseph found grace in his [Potiphar's] sight, and he served him: and he made him overseer over his house, and all that he had he put into his hand" (verse 4). *The Companion Bible* says *served* in this verse means "became his personal servant."[31] Joseph diligently and faithfully served Potiphar as his personal servant and hand. Later, when

---

31 *The Companion Bible, King James Version,* Kregel Publications (Grand Rapids: Kregel, Inc., 1990) "served" p. 56.

he was thrown into prison, Joseph served the prison warden the same way—with diligence and faithfulness. He ended up in charge of both of those places. God not only promoted him, but He made Joseph a prosperous man!

The second part of that verse in Proverbs 12 talks about the opposite kind of person—someone who is slothful. The Hebrew word for *slothful* in verse 24 means "idle, slack."[32] It can also mean "remiss," which the dictionary says means "careless, negligent, or slow in performing one's duty or business." That kind of person, the Bible says, will be under *tribute,* or as the Hebrew word says, "a burden, a tax in the form of forced labor, a task [master]."[33] I don't know about you, but I certainly prefer the rewards of diligence and faithfulness!

The powerful force of faithfulness will even open the door for God to protect you.

Psalm 31:23 says, "The Lord preserveth the faithful." Faithfulness will help you close the door on the devil whose aim is to steal, kill and destroy. It will keep you safe and secure, even in the midst of a dangerous world.

You can see a good example of the rewards of faithfulness by looking at the life of another Old Testament saint, Daniel. He was one of the most faithful men in the Bible. As a teenager, like Joseph, he was carried away from his homeland and taken captive to Babylon. When he got there, he initially worked as a servant in the king's palace. He was so faithful in that position, he kept being promoted, until eventually, he became one of three presidents who ruled directly under the Babylonian king!

---

32 *Strong's Exhaustive Concordance of the Bible,* James Strong (Nashville: Thomas Nelson Publishers, 1984) H7423.
33 Ibid. H4522.

After serving in that office for a while, Daniel was promoted to an even higher position. "Because an excellent spirit was in him" (Daniel 6:3), the king decided to set him over the whole realm. The other two presidents were jealous when Daniel got that promotion. They didn't like the fact that he outranked them, so they set about to undermine and destroy him.

> Then the presidents and princes sought to find occasion against Daniel concerning the kingdom; but they could find none occasion nor fault; forasmuch as he was faithful, neither was there any error or fault found in him. Then said these men, We shall not find any occasion against this Daniel, except we find it against him concerning the law of his God (verses 4-5).

Imagine a politician with so much integrity that no one can dig up one bit of dirt about him! Think of a person of power in public office who is so honest, upright and faithful to his responsibilities that no one can find any fault with him. That's the kind of person Daniel was. Even his worst enemies, try as they might, were unable to dig up any dirt to use against him.

So, what did they do? Knowing Daniel faithfully prayed to God three times a day, they came up with a decree that would make such praying illegal. Then they went to the king and presented it to him.

> King Darius, [they said].... All the presidents of the kingdom, the governors, and the princes, the counsellors, and the captains, have consulted together to establish a royal statute, and to make a firm decree, that whosoever shall ask a petition of any God or man for thirty days, save of thee, O king, he shall be cast into the den of lions. Now, O king, establish the decree, and sign the writing, that it be not changed, according to the law of the Medes and Persians, which altereth not. Wherefore king Darius signed the writing and the decree.

Now when Daniel knew that the writing was signed, he went into his house; and his windows being open in his chamber toward Jerusalem, he kneeled upon his knees three times a day, and prayed, and gave thanks before his God, as he did aforetime (verses 6-10).

Isn't that amazing? Even under threat of death, Daniel continued to be as faithful as ever. He didn't decide to skip his prayer times for the next 30 days. He didn't even try to keep his praying a secret by shutting his windows and praying silently where no one could hear. No, Daniel was going to honor God regardless of what happened. Lions' den or no lions' den, he was going to keep doing exactly what he'd always done because that's what God had told him to do.

Daniel's enemies, of course, reported his behavior to the king and demanded that Daniel be fed to the lions. The king was sorely displeased with himself because he really liked Daniel, but he could find no legal way around it. He had signed a law, made it irrevocable, and now it had to be enforced.

Then the king commanded, and they brought Daniel, and cast him into the den of lions. Now the king spake and said unto Daniel, Thy God whom thou servest continually, he will deliver thee. And a stone was brought, and laid upon the mouth of the den; and the king sealed it with his own signet, and with the signet of his lords; that the purpose might not be changed concerning Daniel. Then the king went to his palace, and passed the night fasting: neither were instruments of musick brought before him: and his sleep went from him. Then the king arose very early in the morning, and went in haste unto the den of lions. And when he came to the den, he cried with a lamentable voice unto Daniel: and the king spake and said to Daniel, O Daniel, servant of the living God, is thy God, whom thou servest continually, able to deliver thee from the lions? Then said Daniel unto the king, O king, live for ever. My God hath sent his angel, and hath shut the lions' mouths, that they have not hurt me: forasmuch as before him innocency was found in me; and also before thee, O king, have I done no hurt. Then was the king exceeding glad for him, and commanded that they should take Daniel up out of the den. So Daniel was taken up out of the den, and no manner of hurt was found upon him, because he believed in his God (verses 16-23).

Have you ever seen a painting of what Daniel sleeping in the lions' den might have looked like? I saw one years ago that impressed me. It showed the lions all gathered peacefully around Daniel, and he was resting his head on one of them, as if the lion were a pillow. I like that image! It shows what I believe to be true: Daniel slept better in the lions' den that night than the king did in the palace!

Why could Daniel sleep so soundly? He was at peace! He knew he'd been faithful to God, and he had confidence that in time of danger, God would be faithful to him.

Sure enough, God not only brought Daniel out of the lions' den unharmed, He caused the tables to be turned on Daniel's enemies, so they could never try to hurt him again:

And the king commanded, and they brought those men which had accused Daniel, and they cast them into the den of lions, them, their children, and their wives; and the lions had the mastery of them, and brake all their bones in pieces or ever they came at the bottom of the den. Then king Darius wrote unto all people, nations, and languages, that dwell in all the earth; Peace be multiplied unto you. I make a decree, That in every dominion of my kingdom men tremble and fear before the God of Daniel: for he is the living God, and stedfast for ever, and his kingdom that which shall not be destroyed, and his dominion shall be even unto the end. He delivereth and rescueth, and he worketh signs and wonders in heaven and in earth, who hath delivered Daniel from the power of the lions. So this Daniel prospered in the reign of Darius, and in the reign of Cyrus the Persian (verses 24-28).

Rewards That Last for Eternity

"But Daniel was an Old Testament prophet!" someone might say. "We can't operate in the kind of faithfulness he did."

Jesus said we can. In fact, He commanded it. In Matthew 24, He spoke to us about preparing for His return:

Therefore be ye also ready: for in such an hour as ye think not the Son of man cometh. Who then is a faithful and wise servant, whom his lord hath made ruler over his household, to give them meat in due season? Blessed is that servant, whom his lord when he cometh shall find so doing. Verily I say unto you, That he shall make him ruler over all his goods. But and if that evil servant shall say in his heart, My lord delayeth his coming; and shall begin to smite his fellowservants, and to eat and drink with the drunken; the lord of that servant shall come in a day when he looketh not for him, and in an hour that he is not aware of, and shall cut him asunder, and appoint him his portion with the hypocrites: there shall be weeping and gnashing of teeth (verses 44-51).

Those verses make it clear: We want to be faithfully serving Jesus and other people when He comes back. If we're doing that when Jesus comes, He said we'll be blessed. We'll not only enjoy the benefits that come with faithfulness in this life, we'll receive rewards that will last for eternity.

When Jesus comes back to the earth to get us, we want Him to find us being faithful! If, on the other hand, He comes back and finds us being unfaithful to Him, our spouses, employers and those He's called us to serve, we'll lose those rewards. Unfaithfulness will rob us of them. Why? Because being unfaithful is being disobedient to God's Word, and disobedience to Him always costs us.

As Proverbs 13:15 says, "the way of the unfaithful is hard" (NKJV). People who take a job and choose to not be faithful to their employer, for example, will have a hard time at that job. If they don't put their whole hearts into it, but instead do as little as they can without getting fired, they'll never be promoted. Their co-workers won't respect them, and they won't enjoy their work or get any satisfaction from it because they're not producing much.

God created us as human beings to produce! He designed us to be industrious and fruitful in whatever we undertake. When we're doing that, we feel good about ourselves. I can go clean the weeds out of a flower bed, and even though it's a simple and unglamorous task, if I really attack those weeds and get rid of them, I can enjoy the fruits of what I did. When I'm finished, I'll feel like I've accomplished something.

That's just the way we are about life. The more we put into our jobs, or other natural things we do, the more we'll get out of them.

The more we put into the things of God, the more we'll receive, and the greater anointing and power we'll walk in.

Jesus taught about this in the parable of the talents in Matthew 25:

> Watch therefore, for ye know neither the day nor the hour wherein the Son of man cometh. For the kingdom of heaven is as a man travelling into a far country, who called his own servants, and delivered unto them his goods. And unto one he

gave five talents, to another two, and to another one; to every man according to his several ability; and straightway took his journey. Then he that had received the five talents went and traded with the same, and made them other five talents. And likewise he that had received two, he also gained other two. But he that had received one went and digged in the earth, and hid his lord's money. After a long time the lord of those servants cometh, and reckoneth with them. And so he that had received five talents came and brought other five talents, saying, Lord, thou deliveredst unto me five talents: behold, I have gained beside them five talents more. His lord said unto him, Well done, thou good and faithful servant: thou hast been faithful over a few things, I will make thee ruler over many things: enter thou into the joy of thy lord. He also that had received two talents came and said, Lord, thou deliveredst unto me two talents: behold, I have gained two other talents beside them. His lord said unto him, Well done, good and faithful servant; thou hast been faithful over a few things, I will make thee ruler over many things: enter thou into the joy of thy lord. Then he which had received the one talent came and said, Lord, I knew thee that thou art an hard man, reaping where thou hast not sown, and gathering where thou hast not strawed: And I was afraid, and went and hid thy talent in the earth: lo, there thou hast that is thine. His lord answered and said unto him, Thou wicked and slothful servant, thou knewest that I reap where I sowed not, and gather where I have not strawed: Thou oughtest therefore to have put my money to the exchangers, and then at my coming I should have received mine own with usury. Take therefore the talent from him, and give it unto him which hath ten talents. For unto every one that hath shall be given, and he shall have abundance: but from him that hath not shall be taken away even that which he hath (verses 13-29).

It's easy to see in that parable how the kingdom of God works. He gives us an assignment, and if we're faithful over it, then He gives us a bigger assignment. He increases and promotes us and, as a result, we experience the joy of the Lord.

If we shrug off our assignments, the opposite happens. We miss out on our opportunities for promotion and experience regret. That's what happened to the wicked servant at the end of the parable. His suffered loss because he behaved unfaithfully.

Why did he behave unfaithfully? Because he didn't really know his master. He thought the man was unfair. He thought His master was a harsh person who reaped where he hadn't sown. Although the master proved to be very fair in how he treated the other two servants, the slothful servant let his lack of faith in the master's goodness stop him from moving out and being faithful. As a result, he ended up going away empty-handed instead of receiving a reward.

The same kind of thing happens today. People don't know the Lord, so they misjudge Him. They get mad at Him and go around saying things like, "God has never done anything for me. He's never helped me. He doesn't care anything about me."

People who make those kinds of statements have a wrong concept of God. They think He's at fault for all the bad things that happen in the world. Because they don't have any understanding of what the Bible says about Him, they're afraid that He's unjust and can't be trusted. Instead of obeying Him, they keep living life their own way, and their lack of faith holds them back from walking in His blessings.

This is why feeding on the Word is so important. It takes faith to respond to God, and Romans 10:17 says it comes by hearing the Word. It also takes faith to be faithful to His call on your life.

When He calls you to do something, in the natural, it often appears impossible. You don't have the resources or ability to do it on your own. So to step out and obey His commands, you must believe He'll back you up with His supernatural power. You must be confident He'll enable you to carry out that assignment and know Him well enough to believe that, in the end, being faithful to Him won't cost you—it will pay!

The Little Things Matter

Think about the confidence in God that's required to be faithful to Him in the area of finances, for instance. It takes faith to be a tither! Most of us, when we first start walking with God, don't see how we can afford to give Him 10% of our income. It looks to us like we'd go under if we did that because we're barely getting by on 100%!

As we read the Bible, however, and we're honest, we'll admit that God's plan is clear. He has called us to tithe. It isn't just an option. We're not supposed to ask ourselves, "Do I really want to tithe?" No, according to the Scriptures, the first 10% of our increase *belongs* to God, and if we aren't obedient to that Word, Malachi 3:8-10 says we're robbing Him.

The reason God set up the tithe was for our sakes, not because He wants to take our money. When we tithe, it allows Him to fulfill for us the promise He made in Malachi 3:10: "Bring ye all the tithes into the storehouse, that there may be meat in mine house, and prove me now herewith...if I will not open you the windows of heaven, and pour you out a blessing, that there shall not be room enough to receive it."

Faithful tithing gives God the opportunity to partner with us financially and cause us to increase.

When Ken and I were first born again, tithing was a big challenge for us. Even though we really wanted to obey God, it took us a while to stick with His financial program. We'd tithe for a while, then decide we needed the money more than God did, and we'd fall by the wayside. As a result, our finances stayed the same. We didn't increase at all.

God kept working with us, though. He kept bringing us back to what the Word says until faith rose up in our hearts, and we made a quality decision. We decided that even if we couldn't buy groceries, we would give God His 10% right off the top. We agreed to not touch that money because it was devoted to Him.

Once we became faithful with the tithe, our finances began to increase. We found we could do more on the 90% than we'd previously been able to do with 100%. What's more, our income began to go up. We also began to experience greater blessing in other areas of our lives because it's a scriptural principle.

When you're faithful to God with your finances, you become more faithful to Him in other ways. When you start putting Him first place on a broader scale, it opens the door for Him to do bigger things for you in every area of life.

The reverse is also true. When you're unfaithful to God in the area of finances, you're unfaithful to Him in other areas. You start putting the things of the world before the things of God, and that prevents Him from being able to trust you with His greater blessings.

Jesus taught about this in Luke 16:10-13:

> He who is faithful in a very little [thing] is faithful also in much, and he who is dishonest and unjust in a very little [thing] is dishonest and unjust also in much. Therefore if you have not been faithful in the [case of] unrighteous mammon (deceitful riches, money, possessions), who will entrust to you the true riches? And if you have not proved faithful in that which belongs to another [whether God or man], who will give you that which is your own [that is, the true riches]? No

servant is able to serve two masters; for either he will hate the one and love the other, or he will stand by and be devoted to the one and despise the other. You cannot serve God and mammon (riches, or anything in which you trust and on which you rely) (AMPC).

Notice that Jesus spoke not only about the importance of being faithful to God where finances are concerned, but He also spoke about being faithful in handling what belongs to other people. He said that if you don't take care of their things, you won't be entrusted with your own. That means, if you want more nice things to enjoy, you need to check up on how you're treating the resources of others.

How well are you caring for the equipment that belongs to your employer, for instance? Are you treating the desk, truck or whatever else your employer has provided you, with respect? Are you treating them as if you had to pay for their upkeep and repair out of your own pocket?

If you're believing for a home of your own, but right now you're still renting, how well are you taking care of your rental house or apartment? Are you being careless with it and tearing it up, or are you treating it as if it belonged to you?

Those are important questions because your faithfulness in such matters has everything to do with your increase!

If you're believing for a better job, set yourself up for increase by being faithful in the job you have. If you want to be a brain surgeon but right now you're waiting tables and saving money so that you can go to school, wait on those tables the very best you can. Even though it might seem like a little thing to you, Jesus told us to be faithful in the little things. So, be a blessing to everyone who comes into that restaurant.

The more faithful you are, the more you'll get people's attention.

Faithfulness grows as you practice it. Like all the other fruit of the spirit, the more you yield to it, the more it flows. Whether you're waiting tables or doing brain surgery, if you're faithful, you'll be noticed and rewarded because out there in the world, faithfulness is rare. When people encounter it, they appreciate and reward it. Employers who find a faithful employee are likely to promote him or her. Customers served faithfully are likely to respond positively in return.

You know what it's like to go into a restaurant where the person who waits on you is unhappy and unfaithful in his or her job. You don't enjoy it very much. Rather than smiling at you when taking your order, you're treated like you're a burden. You might hear an impatient, "What do you want to eat?" and then, "There it is," when it's brought to your table.

When the meal is over and it's time to pay the check, you don't really want to give that waiter or waitress much of a tip, do you? You might give them something just out of obligation, but you don't really feel motivated to bless that person in a big way.

It's a whole different experience, however, when you go into a restaurant and the person who waits on you does it with faithfulness. He or she is happy and cheerful, glad to see you and do you good. The person keeps your water glass filled and watches your table to see if you need anything.

Ken and I really like those kinds of waiters and waitresses! We have a few of them in our area, and we try to seek them out because they're always upbeat. They're always ready to laugh and eager to know what they can do for us. Some of them call us "honey." (We live in Texas, and it's friendly here!) They serve us with so much joy, you'd think we were family.

We really enjoy tipping those waiters and waitresses! Of course, we tip the grumpy ones too (because we love the Lord and want to be a blessing to everyone). But the waiters and waitresses who usually come out the best financially, not just with us but other customers as well, are those who are dedicated and wholehearted in their work.

Those waiters and waitresses are the ones who are faithful.

Keep Swimming Upstream

"But Gloria," you might say, "sometimes the people I work for don't even notice when I'm faithful. They don't reward me for it at all."

No matter what your line of work might be, Jesus is really the One you're serving. So put your confidence in Him, knowing He will notice and reward you. Just keep following the instructions in the New Testament:

> Servants, obey in everything those who are your earthly masters, not only when their eyes are on you as pleasers of men, but in simplicity of purpose [with all your heart] because of your reverence for the Lord and as a sincere expression of your devotion to Him. Whatever may be your task, work at it heartily (from the soul), as [something done] for the Lord and not for men, knowing [with all certainty] that it is from the Lord [and not from men] that you will receive the inheritance which is your [real] reward. [The One Whom] you are actually serving [is] the Lord Christ (the Messiah) (Colossians 3:22-24, AMPC).
>
> Servants (slaves), be obedient to those who are your physical masters, having respect for them and eager concern to please them, in singleness of motive and with all your heart, as [service] to Christ [Himself]— not in the way of eye-service [as if they were watching you] and only to please men, but as servants (slaves) of Christ, doing the will of God heartily and with your whole soul; rendering service readily with goodwill, as to the Lord and not to men, knowing that for whatever

good anyone does, he will receive his reward from the Lord, whether he is slave or free (Ephesians 6:5-8, AMPC).

Can you imagine what would happen if believers started obeying these verses? People would sit up and take notice! They'd begin paying more attention to the Church because in this sin-darkened, secular world, faithfulness is such a rare commodity.

The way of the world is to be *un*faithful—to do as little as you can get away with—on the job or in your relationships with others. The way of the world is to forget about honor, commitment and loyalty and just do whatever you want to do. For instance, in the world's system, if you give your word to someone or sign a contract and then decide later you don't want to honor it, you get a lawyer to get you out of it. He finds a way out for you to legally break your word and violate the contract. The other person is left with your broken promise, and you walk away without regret.

That has become the accepted way of life. It's so widely accepted, in fact, that it can even affect the Church. Because we're surrounded by the spirit of unfaithfulness, if we don't maintain our union with the Lord and just go with the flow of the world, we too can be influenced by that same worldly spirit.

We have to swim upstream against that tide to walk continually in faithfulness. We have to feed on what the Word says about it and make a commitment.

Speak Your Faith

I'm going to obey the Word of God. I will be faithful to my spouse, family, friends and employer. When I'm tempted to be unfaithful, I'm going to turn down that temptation because I'm a believer and, for me, being unfaithful is wrong!

"But Gloria," you might say, "Do you really think I have the power to keep that commitment?"

Absolutely! After all, you don't have to do it in your own natural strength. You have the faithfulness of your faithful heavenly Father working in you and through you. He is backing you up with His own supernatural power every step of the way!

The Apostle Paul wrote in 1 Corinthians 7:25 that he had "obtained mercy of the Lord to be faithful." As a joint heir with Jesus, you have obtained that same mercy. So receive it by faith, and put it to work.

Whatever your situation in life, yield to faithfulness in the midst of it. Be faithful to the Lord and to the people around you. Be faithful in spiritual things and in natural things. In return, you will surely receive, from the Lord Himself, His richest rewards!

Chapter 13

THE WINNING FORCE
OF MEEKNESS

*But the meek shall inherit the earth; and shall
delight themselves in the abundance of peace.*

PSALM 37:11

Remember what it used to be like in gym class when all the kids divided up into teams to play a game? There was always one scrawny, unathletic member of the class who wound up being the last one picked because none of the teams thought he or she could help them win.

When it comes to the fruit of the spirit, that's how it is with meekness. When believers choose the fruit they want to cultivate, meekness tends to get left standing on the sidelines because most Christians associate it with weakness. They think of it as going around with your head down, not looking anyone in the eye, and letting the whole world run over you. They think having meekness on their team would keep them from ever really winning in life.

The reality is just the opposite! Meekness isn't weakness, it's strength! It's strength of the highest caliber. It's strength that's been brought into submission to divine authority. Meekness is power under such perfect control that even when under tremendous pressure, it remains gentle and loving.

A powerhouse force of the spirit, meekness is essential to the making of an overcomer. When we think of what it takes to be victorious, meekness should be one of the first things that comes to mind!

The word *meek* is defined by Webster as "humbly patient under provocation from others...submissive...gentle and kind." Its synonyms include: "forbearing, yielding, unassuming, calm, soft."

Alexander Maclaren says, "Meekness...points to a submissiveness of spirit which does not lift itself up against oppositions, but bends like a reed before the storm."[34] It gives you the strength to trust God to take care of the situation, so you don't have to fight for your own way. Yet at the same time, it doesn't make you a pushover. When something arises that needs to be dealt with, meekness gives you the spiritual backbone to stand up and do what needs to be done.

You can see an example of this in the life of the Apostle Paul. He preached meekness and practiced it, yet he boldly confronted the legalists who tried to twist the gospel. He strongly opposed them and wrote in Galatians 2:5 that he gave them no place by subjection, "no, not for an hour"!

> *Although meekness is gentle and patient, it doesn't just lie down and play dead when confronted with evil.*

Meekness can be firm. But even when it's firm, it operates in love. Actually, meekness and love have so much in common that in 1 Corinthians 13 the two words are interchangeable. You can say with all accuracy:

---

34   Maclaren, "The Fruit of the Spirit" in *Expositions of Holy Scripture*.

Meekness endures long and is patient and kind; it's never envious nor boils over with jealousy, is not boastful or vainglorious, does not display itself haughtily. It is not conceited (arrogant and inflated with pride). Meekness does not insist on its own rights or its own way, for it is not self-seeking; it is not touchy or fretful or resentful; it takes no account of the evil done to it [it pays no attention to a suffered wrong]. It does not rejoice at injustice and unrighteousness, but rejoices when right and truth prevail. It bears up under anything and everything that comes, is ever ready to believe the best of every person, its hopes are fadeless under all circumstances, and it endures everything [without weakening]. Like love, meekness never fails (adapted from verses 4-8, AMPC).

Teachable and Receptive to Correction

In addition to helping in your relationships with people, meekness helps you in your relationship with God. Having a submissive heart toward Him helps you to respond to Him and keeps you receptive to new things He shows you in the Word, for instance.

If you're lacking in meekness, when God reveals something to you that contradicts what you've always been taught, you'll be resistant. Rather than acknowledging you've been wrong and agreeing with Him, you'll cling to your old ways of thinking. You'll say, "Well, that's just not the way I was taught."

Meekness will help you to repent when the Lord corrects you, instead of arguing with Him and resisting a change in your behavior—especially if you don't want to do what He's telling you. It will help you follow His leading and not just go right on doing what your flesh wants to do.

If you've been holding a grudge against someone, for example, and God shows you in His Word that you're required to forgive, you might not want to do that. Your flesh might still be angry with that person. It might be saying, "I don't want to forgive. That person did me wrong!"

In a situation like that, meekness will come to your aid! It will help you obey God and maintain a teachable spirit before Him. It will cause you to submit to His commands and follow His directions while keeping your ears open to His voice so you can hear and do what He says.

Study the life of Jesus, and you'll see what I mean. He yielded continually to meekness while He was on the earth. That's why he was able to fulfill His divine calling. He was so meek toward God that there was never the slightest breech in the fellowship they had with one another. He submitted to God's will so completely and continuously that He could say, "I do always those things that please him" (John 8:29).

"But Gloria," you might say, "Jesus could say that because He's sinless and perfect. He pleased God because He *is* God!"

Yes, He is. But remember, He didn't operate as God during His earth walk. When He took upon Himself flesh, He laid aside His divine privileges and lived His life as a man. Philippians 2:5-8 says:

> Let this same attitude and purpose and [humble] mind be in
> you which was in Christ Jesus: [Let Him be your example in
> humility:] who, although being essentially one with God and
> in the form of God [possessing the fullness of the attributes
> which make God God], did not think this equality with God
> was a thing to be eagerly grasped or retained, but stripped
> Himself [of all privileges and rightful dignity], so as to assume
> the guise of a servant (slave), in that He became like men and
> was born a human being. And after He had appeared in
> human form, He abased and humbled Himself [still further]
> and carried His obedience to the extreme of death, even the
> death of the cross! *(AMPC)*.

We don't often think about this, but Jesus grew up in God the same way you and I do. He prayed and dedicated Himself to God, and He spent time in the Word. He submitted Himself to everything God said to Him, both through the written Word and by the voice of the Holy Spirit. As a man, Jesus had a will of His own and the ability to make His own choices, yet He said to God in every circumstance, "Thy will be done" (Matthew 6:10, 26:42; Luke 11:2).

That wasn't always easy for Him, either. Obedience to God required Him to say no to His flesh just as we have to do. It required Him to bring His personal will into subjection to the Father even when He knew that doing so would take Him through some hard places. As Hebrews 5:8 says, "Though he were a Son, yet learned he obedience by the things which he suffered."

In the Garden of Gethsemane, for instance, Jesus didn't want to go to the cross and be separated from the Father. He didn't want to be made sin with the sin of the whole world. He said to God, "If there's any way, let this cup pass from me" (Matthew 26:39). Yet when God made it clear there was no other way, He obeyed. He yielded to the force of meekness and said, "Not my will, but thine, be done" (Luke 22:42).

Jesus already paid the price for Adam's sin on the cross, so none of us will ever be required to do anything as hard as what Jesus did on Calvary. But at times in our walk with God, we'll all have to make sacrifices. Sometimes, He may ask us to do things we'd rather not do.

He might give us a ministry assignment that puts a greater demand on our time or resources than we'd like (as He did when He told Ken and me to go on daily television). He might ask us to sacrifice an hour of sleep and spend an extra hour in prayer every morning. He might prompt us to share the gospel with a person we're reluctant to approach.

God has different plans for each of us. But whatever He asks us to do, the fruit of meekness will help us do it! It will help us to be obedient to the Lord, not only in big ways but in the small things, the little details of life.

I remember one time, for example, Ken wanted me to learn a certain skill. It was something he thought was interesting and important, but it didn't interest me at all. For a while, I resisted. I kept putting it off and hoping Ken would just forget about it. But after a while, the Lord spoke to me and said, *I want you to do that.*

On my own, I would never have chosen to invest my time that way. Yet once the Lord let me know it would please Him, I let meekness come to my aid. I obeyed, and as it turned out, that skill became a great blessing to me.

That's the way it always is when you obey the Lord. Everything He tells you to do ultimately turns out to be a blessing. By the same token, every time you resist His commands, you miss out on something wonderful and wind up experiencing regret.

Proverbs 12:1 says, "Whoever loves instruction loves knowledge, but he who hates correction is stupid" (NKJV). So, meekness keeps us from being stupid, as this Bible version says!

Meekness makes us wise because it causes us to be receptive to the correction of God.

Meekness will even help us get more out of going to church and keep us from getting irritated when the minister says something that convicts us. It will stop us from becoming offended and thinking he is intentionally criticizing us—that he's singling us out and "reading our mail."

In most cases, when that kind of thing happens in church, the minister doesn't have anyone specific in mind at all. He's just speaking by the leading of the Lord. He may not even realize the Holy Spirit is zeroing in on an area of disobedience in someone's life, identifying something that person needs to change and telling them, in a very personal way, exactly what they need to hear.

Maybe the minister is preaching about the tithe, and some of the people in the congregation haven't been tithing. Instead of yielding to meekness and agreeing with what the Holy Spirit is saying, sometimes those people will get mad at the preacher. All he's doing is telling them what the Word says! He is giving them instruction from the Lord that would bring them great financial blessing. Yet instead of receiving that instruction and positioning themselves to receive a blessing, they get upset and refuse it.

As Proverbs 12:1 says, that's stupid! So, don't do it. Yield to meekness, and submit to God in everything. Whatever He tells you to do, whether directly or through one of His ministers, it's for your good and your increase. He's good, and He wants to do you good. So obey, so that THE BLESSING is unhindered!

The Meekest Man on Earth

I like what W.E. Vine teaches about meekness. In his commentary, he says:

> [Meekness is] an inwrought grace of the soul; the exercises of it are first and chiefly towards God. It is that temper of spirit in which we accept His dealings with us as good, and therefore without disputing or resisting; it is closely linked with the word tapeinophrosunē [humility]...it is only the humble heart which is also the meek, and which, as such, does not fight against God and more or less struggle and contend with Him.
>
> The meaning of praütēs "is not readily expressed in English, for the terms meekness, mildness, commonly used, suggest weakness and pusillanimity [timidity, cowardice], to a greater or less extent, whereas praütēs does nothing of the kind.... [It]

describes a condition of mind and heart, and as 'gentleness' is appropriate rather to actions.... It must be clearly understood, therefore, that the meekness manifested by the Lord and commended to the believer is the fruit of power. The common assumption is that when a man is meek it is because he cannot help himself; but the Lord was 'meek' because He had the infinite resources of God at His command."[35]

Take a moment and think about what was said there about Jesus: He was the picture of meekness, yet He was never without power! He was in control the whole time He walked the earth. He walked through every situation as a Master yet, at the same time, always operated in love, humility and gentleness.

Jesus never fought for His own rights because He didn't have to. He had the power of God moving in and for Him all the time. Until He got ready to lay down His life on the Cross, Satan couldn't even touch Him. Because Jesus did whatever God commanded, God always did whatever Jesus asked!

According to *Vine's Expository Dictionary of Biblical Words,* meekness is "the opposite of self-assertiveness and self-interest; it is equanimity [stability or composure] of spirit that is neither elated nor cast down, simply because it is not occupied with self at all."[36]

When we're walking in meekness, we can get ourselves off our minds!

We don't have to be self-assertive and fight with other people to get our way. Instead, we can just do whatever God says, letting Him see to it

---

35 *Vine's Expository Dictionary of Biblical Words,* "meek, meekness," *praütēs* or *praotes,* 401.
36 Ibid., 401.

that things work out for us and trusting His power to work on our behalf. We can rely on Him to take our part and make sure we're protected and not run over.

This is how Moses operated in the Old Testament. Meekness was his most outstanding characteristic. In the natural, he might have been described as having a gentle personality. But, according to the Bible, there was a spiritual reason he was like that. It was because "the man Moses was very meek, above all the men which were upon the face of the earth" (Numbers 12:3).

Meekness isn't what most of us would look for if we were recruiting a leader to go up against Pharaoh and his army! If we needed someone to call down the power of God and bring the most powerful nation in the world to its knees, we probably wouldn't choose the meekest man in the whole earth. Yet that's exactly what God did because He knew Moses' humble, submissive spirit would make him cooperative. It would cause him to do what God told him to do.

Unlike some people, Moses wasn't a legend in his own mind. He wasn't self-confident and impressed with his own abilities. He didn't think He was smarter than God and stubbornly insist on doing things his own way. On the contrary! Moses didn't have much confidence in himself at all. When God initially called him, herding sheep on the backside of the desert, he thought he was too weak to deal with Pharaoh. He asked God to find someone else to do it. "I can't even speak well!" he said.

God wasn't looking for speaking ability, however, so He overrode Moses' protests. He chose him anyway, not because he was the most outgoing person, but because of his meekness. which, far from being a weakness, was Moses' greatest strength.

Moses' meekness is what made him a good leader for the Israelites. It's what enabled him to deal with them firmly, while at the same time continuing to be gentle with them. Over the 40 years he led them through the wilderness, they regularly rebelled against his leadership, yet he repeatedly refused to get into strife with them. Even when they opposed and criticized him, he trusted God to defend him. Rather than fighting for his own rights, Moses stayed focused on others' well-being.

From a Family Feud to an Intercessory Prayer Meeting

One time, Moses' own brother and sister even came against him. They questioned his judgment, criticized him in a very personal way, and even opposed him—all because they didn't think he married the right woman. In most families, that would cause trouble for generations! Everyone would split up and take sides because, in the natural, if a man's family rejects his wife, there are only three options for him. He can: 1) get rid of her, 2) fight with his family, or 3) stay away from them altogether.

Because Moses walked in meekness, however, he had another option. He didn't have to fight back or argue with his brother and sister. He could respond with gentleness and look to God to handle things. So, that's what he did. When they challenged his position before God, he just stayed quiet.

What happened as a result?

> Immediately the Lord called to Moses, Aaron, and Miriam and said, "Go out to the Tabernacle, all three of you!" And the three of them went out. Then the Lord descended in the pillar of cloud and stood at the entrance of the Tabernacle. "Aaron and Miriam!" he called, and they stepped forward. And the Lord said to them, "Now listen to me! Even with prophets, I the Lord communicate by visions and dreams. But that is not how I communicate with my servant Moses. He is entrusted with my entire house. I speak to him face to face, directly and not in riddles! He sees the Lord as he is. Should

you not be afraid to criticize him?" The Lord was furious with them, and he departed. As the cloud moved from above the Tabernacle, Miriam suddenly became white as snow with leprosy (Numbers 12:4-10, NLT-96).

It just doesn't pay to come against the servant of God! You don't want to go around criticizing a man or woman who belongs to Him. It doesn't matter if that person is one of your family members or not. If you don't like something he or she is doing, pray for that person. But don't set yourself up as judge.

Nobody's paying you to judge! Nobody's called you to do that except the devil, and you don't want to answer his call. You want to obey the Lord, and He said in the Scriptures, "Touch not mine anointed, and do my prophets no harm" (1 Chronicles 16:22).

This was serious business. Miriam opened herself up to leprosy when she came against Moses!

When Aaron saw what had happened, he cried out to Moses, "Oh, my lord! Please don't punish us for this sin we have so foolishly committed. Don't let her be like a stillborn baby, already decayed at birth." So Moses cried out to the Lord, "Heal her, O God, I beg you!" (Numbers 12:10-13, NLT-96).

If he hadn't walked in meekness, Moses might have reacted differently to that situation. He may have decided to let Miriam suffer for a while before he prayed for her. Or, he might have said, "Well, I'm sorry you have leprosy, but that's just tough. I'm the man of God, and you shouldn't have talked that way about my wife. You got what you deserve!"

But that's not how Moses responded. He didn't spend a single second nursing his hurt feelings. He didn't think about himself at all. He was only concerned about Miriam. He had so much compassion on her that

he immediately cried out to God on her behalf and asked Him to
heal her.

That's the kind of compassion you and I ought to have in such situations. As born-again believers living under the new covenant, we ought to
be at least as gentle and forgiving as Moses was under the old covenant! If
one of our family members does us wrong, we ought to keep right on loving them. We ought not to get angry and decide to have nothing to do
with them. If we do that, we'll open the door to the devil to come into
our lives.

We can't hold grudges against people and do well in life.

Neither can we prosper in God spiritually, physically, financially or
any other way, when we're in strife. So, if you've been fighting with your
family members, repent and let the fruit of meekness flow out of you
toward them. Be like Moses and cry out to the Lord on behalf of the people who've been giving you problems. Say, "Lord, help them! Heal them!
Forgive us all, and make this situation right!"

Complainers and Controllers

Moses not only walked in meekness where his family was concerned, but
he did it in his relationships with others, as well. He prayed and interceded
for everyone in Israel, even though they were continually causing
him trouble.

Take, for instance, the time the Israelites refused to go into the
Promised Land. That situation was an absolute mess. No matter what
Moses said, the Israelites wouldn't listen to him. Instead, they listened to
the 10 unbelieving spies who returned from their expedition into the land
and told the people, "There are giants over there! The cities have huge

walls and the people are fierce. There's no way we can defeat them. We're like grasshoppers in their eyes!" (Numbers 13:28-33).

The only two people who sided with Moses in that situation were Joshua and Caleb. Although they'd gone into the land and seen the giants too, unlike the other spies, they reminded the Israelites of the promises God had given through Moses and tried to encourage the people. "We have God on our side!" they said. "He'll give us the victory! He'll back us up in battle and give us this land!" (Numbers 14:6-9).

The Israelites, however, clung to their unbelief. They not only refused to be encouraged, they got mad at Moses and wanted to stone Joshua and Caleb (verses 2, 4, 10)!

I've noticed, over the years, that kind of thing happens even today. When people get into unbelief, they want to be mad at someone for it. They don't ever want to think, *It's my fault. I'm the one who's not believing God.* They want to blame the pastor, the TV preacher, their mother—anyone but themselves.

That's what the Israelites did in this situation. They cried and wept and "their voices rose in a great chorus of complaint against Moses."

> "We wish we had died in Egypt, or even here in the wilderness!" they wailed. "Why is the Lord taking us to this country only to have us die in battle? Our wives and little ones will be carried off as slaves! Let's get out of here and return to Egypt!" Then they plotted among themselves, "Let's choose a leader and go back to Egypt!" (verses 2-4, NLT-96).

How did Moses respond to all this?

He prayed! Rather than getting angry and resentful, he and Aaron "fell face down on the ground before the people of Israel" and called on the Lord (verse 5, NLT-96).

This is something for us to learn. If we'll allow meekness to flow in our lives, we won't retaliate when people say bad things about us, blame us and find fault with what we do. We won't strike back at them and say things like, "Well, you're not so perfect yourself!" and then list a few of their faults. We won't even try to convince them we're right and try to make ourselves look good.

No, if we're walking in meekness, we'll just fall on our faces before God and turn the situation over to Him.

God can handle anyone who comes against you! It doesn't matter whether you're being maligned by just a couple of relatives or being plotted against by literally millions of people.

If you'll respond with gentleness and depend on God, He can and will defend you.

One time, God even protected Moses from a group of rebellious preachers! He defended him against a Levite named Korah who decided he had as much a right to lead Israel as Moses did and got a group of his buddies to agree with him.

> They incited a rebellion against Moses, involving 250 other prominent leaders, all members of the assembly. They went to Moses and Aaron and said, "You have gone too far! Everyone in Israel has been set apart by the Lord, and he is with all of us. What right do you have to act as though you are greater than anyone else among all these people of the Lord?" (Numbers 16:2-4, NLT-96).

You can tell just from what those Levites said in those verses that they had everything backward. Moses hadn't acted as though he was greater than anyone else. He hadn't lifted himself up over the people of Israel. God is the One who gave Moses his position. Moses didn't even want the job! He didn't consider himself qualified and tried to talk God into finding someone else.

It was Korah and his bunch who were full of pride. They weren't content to just take whatever place the Lord gave them. They wanted the top position. Rather than submitting to the one God put in charge, they wanted to be the boss!

Really, it's people fighting over who gets to be the boss that's behind most of the strife in the world. That's also what's behind most of the marriage problems, and it's what causes church fusses and splits. It's what triggers wars between nations. Time and again, fights erupt because people on both sides are vying for control.

The force of meekness will keep you out of such fights. It will save your marriage and help prevent that split in your church. It will help bring peace to an entire nation.

Meekness certainly would have helped Korah and his friends! If they'd been walking in meekness, it would have come to their rescue. It would have kept them submissive to God and made them content to stay in their places.

Instead, they got themselves into a dangerous position. They wound up on the wrong side of God because, as usual, Moses turned the situation over to Him. Rather than fighting for control and seeking retribution:

> ...he threw himself down with his face to the ground. Then he said to Korah and his followers, "Tomorrow morning the Lord will show us who belongs to him and who is holy. The Lord will allow those who are chosen to enter his holy presence. You, Korah, and all your followers must do this: Take incense burners, and burn incense in them tomorrow before the Lord. Then we will see whom the Lord chooses as his holy one" (verses 4-7, NLT-96).

In other words, Moses said to those who were rebelling against him, "Let's just put this in the hands of God, and let Him decide. Let's go before Him, and if He chooses you, then I'll step aside and let you lead the people."

Truth be told, Moses might have wished God would choose Korah. He might have been delighted at the thought of someone else taking over the responsibility of leading that nation full of cantankerous people. But that wasn't Moses' choice to make. God was the One who had appointed him. So, Moses decided he and Korah would go together before the Lord and let Him make the call.

Korah's group, however, didn't like that plan. When Moses presented it to them, they replied:

> "We refuse to come! Isn't it enough that you brought us out of Egypt, a land flowing with milk and honey, to kill us here in this wilderness, and that you now treat us like your subjects? What's more, you haven't brought us into the land flowing with milk and honey or given us an inheritance of fields and vineyards. Are you trying to fool us? We will not come." Then Moses became very angry and said to the Lord, "Do not accept their offerings! I have not taken so much as a donkey from them, and I have never hurt a single one of them" (verses 12-15, NLT-96).

Notice in this instance, Moses got angry. So obviously, being meek doesn't mean you never feel anger. It means you handle that feeling the way God commands. He said, "Be ye angry, and sin not" (Ephesians 4:26), and that's what Moses did here. He didn't sin by spewing his wrath out onto other people. He dealt with his emotions by talking to the Lord.

That's a good example to follow. When you get angry, go to God about it. He can do you some good. If you respond in anger to other people, they'll get angry in return, and the fight will be on. But if you'll look to God, He can enable you to come out a winner without you ever having to fight.

He certainly did that for Moses. When Korah and his band of rebels came with their incense burners and stood at the entrance of the Tabernacle with Moses and Aaron:

> Then the glorious presence of the Lord appeared to the whole community, and the Lord said to Moses and Aaron, "Get away from these people so that I may instantly destroy them!" But Moses and Aaron fell face down on the ground. "O God, the God and source of all life," they pleaded. "Must you be angry with all the people when only one man sins?" And the Lord said to Moses, "Then tell all the people to get away from the tents of Korah, Dathan, and Abiram." So Moses got up and rushed over to the tents of Dathan and Abiram, followed closely by the Israelite leaders. "Quick!" he told the people. "Get away from the tents of these wicked men, and don't touch anything that belongs to them. If you do, you will be destroyed for their sins." So all the people stood back from the tents of Korah, Dathan, and Abiram. Then Dathan and Abiram came out and stood at the entrances of their tents with their wives and children and little ones. And Moses said, "By this you will know that the Lord has sent me to do all these things that I have done—for I have not done them on my own. If these men die a natural death, then the Lord has not sent me. But if the Lord performs a miracle and the ground opens up and swallows them and all their belongings, and they go down alive into the grave, then you will know that these men have despised the Lord." He had hardly finished speaking the words when the ground suddenly split open beneath them. The earth opened up and swallowed the men, along with their households and the followers who were standing with them,

and everything they owned. So they went down alive into the grave, along with their belongings. The earth closed over them, and they all vanished. All of the people of Israel fled as they heard their screams, fearing that the earth would swallow them, too (verses 19-34, NLT-96).

Even in that potentially volatile situation, Moses didn't do one thing to fight for his rights! On the contrary, He fell on his face before the Lord on behalf of the Israelites who had gotten mixed up with those rebels. He asked God to have mercy on them.

> *When you are walking in meekness, you forgive and pray for those who have done you wrong.*

When you allow the fruit of meekness to flow out of your spirit, you forgive and intercede for those people before God. You can't forgive and pray for someone and stay mad at that person at the same time. So, when you yield to meekness, it keeps you out of strife and bitterness. It keeps you free!

Know-It-Alls Don't Listen

Meekness has all kinds of other benefits, too! Psalm 22:26 says, for example, "The meek shall eat and be satisfied." When you're satisfied, everything is all right. Things are working for you, and you're aren't lacking anything. That's a great way to live, and it's one of the blessings that comes with being a gentle, meek person.

Psalm 25:9 says, "The meek will [the Lord] guide in judgment: and the meek will he teach his way." When you're meek, God can guide you and teach you because you'll listen to Him. You'll submit to Him and do what He says, instead of trying to tell Him you have a better way.

Ken and I started learning how much wiser it is to submit to God's way in our early days of ministry. The first thing God told us to do was to move to Tulsa so that Ken could go to Oral Roberts University. We didn't see any way in the natural how we could afford to do that. We were already financially broke and in debt. If we went to Tulsa, a city where Ken didn't have a job, it looked to us like we wouldn't have enough money even to eat!

We didn't know then what we know now about faith and the Word of God so, for a while, we debated about what we should do. The longer we debated, the more we went downhill financially. The more broke we became, the more impossible moving to Tulsa and enrolling Ken in school appeared to be.

Eventually, though, we did it—and, of course, God made a way for us. He took care of us and provided for us. Best of all, because we were doing what He said to do, He was able to teach us how to walk in THE BLESSING.

We might have never learned to prosper had we not been meek before God and obeyed Him. We might have never found our way into His plan for our lives had we not been willing to humble ourselves and do things His way—even when it looked to us like it wouldn't work out for our good. That's what opened the door to all the blessings of God we're enjoying today. It's what opened the door for us to experience for ourselves the truth of verses like these:

> The meek shall inherit the earth; and shall delight themselves in the abundance of peace (Psalm 37:11).
>
> The Lord lifteth up the meek (Psalm 147:6).
>
> The meek also shall increase their joy in the Lord, and the poor among men shall rejoice in the Holy One of Israel (Isaiah 29:19).

God would teach every person on earth how to prosper if they'd just be meek enough to allow Him to do it! It's His will that all men be saved and blessed by coming into the knowledge of the truth (1 Timothy 2:4). But if people won't listen to Him and be teachable and submissive, then God can't get them the answers they need.

This is the reason, as Isaiah 61:1 says, the Spirit of the Lord was upon Jesus, "to preach good tidings unto the meek." The meek were the ones who would listen to Him! The religious know-it-alls of Jesus' day were too proud. They considered themselves experts in the things of God, so they just wanted to argue with Jesus. They wanted to let Him know He was wrong because His teachings were crosswise to the religious traditions they'd always believed.

However, Jesus was speaking the very words of God! He was saying only what He heard from His Father. Yet the "experts" refused to listen. The meek, on the other hand, were all ears! Hungry to receive from God, they humbled themselves like little children, came to hear Jesus, and were BLESSED AND HEALED!

That's the way you and I want to be. We don't want to be like the so-called experts. We want to be humble before God. We want to be pliable, teachable, and ready to receive and agree with His Word so God can give us His wisdom and bring to pass in our lives the promise in Matthew 5:5: "Blessed are the meek: for they shall inherit the earth."

Jesus, As Approachable As Ever

Like the other fruit of the spirit, meekness is already inside us as believers because we have Jesus inside us. And as we've already seen, He is perfectly meek. He's meek toward God, and He's also meek toward people.

That's why people always flocked around Him when He was ministering on the earth. His meekness made Him approachable. It kept people from being intimidated by Him.

As God in the flesh, if Jesus hadn't wrapped Himself in meekness, He would have been *un*approachable. He would have seemed so far above other people that they would have thought, *Oh, we can't come into His presence. He's too great. He's too famous.*

Jesus, however, didn't come across that way. He never acted like He was so important and so much above everyone that He was unapproachable. He was gentle and humble. People loved Him. Little children, rather than being afraid of Him, wanted to get close to Him. Even notorious sinners who'd been rejected by the religious leaders of the day wanted to be near Him. (One even invited Him to his house for dinner: See Luke 19:1-10.) People of all kinds felt so accepted by Jesus that multitudes responded when He said:

> Come to Me, all you who labor and are heavy-laden and over-burdened, and I will cause you to rest. [I will ease and relieve and refresh your souls.] Take My yoke upon you and learn of Me, for I am gentle (meek) and humble (lowly) in heart, and you will find rest (relief and ease and refreshment and recreation and blessed quiet) for your souls. For My yoke is wholesome (useful, good—not harsh, hard, sharp, or pressing, but comfortable, gracious, and pleasant), and My burden is light and easy to be borne (Matthew 11:28-30, AMPC).

You can see from those verses the kind of personality Jesus had when He was on earth. He was kind. He wasn't harsh or hard or sharp or pressing. He was so gracious and pleasant to be with that He couldn't go anywhere without people coming around, wanting to be with Him.

Why did Jesus have that kind of personality? Because He's like His Father, and the Father is good (John 14:9).

Most people didn't know much about God's goodness when Jesus was ministering on the earth. But Jesus came with the love of God. He showed them that God is good, and His mercy endures forever.

Jesus is revealing the same things to us today. He's still approachable as ever, and He still says to us when we find ourselves heavy-laden or over-burdened, "Come to Me! I'll destroy that yoke off your neck. I'll give you ease and refresh your soul!"

Even when we make the worst mistakes and sin, knowing better than to do it, if we'll come to Jesus, He is always an advocate for us with the Father (1 John 2:1). He never turns us away. He never says, "Well, I'm not helping you this time. You got yourself into this mess; now you get yourself out."

No, that's not how Jesus is. He's still meek. He still receives us, no matter what we've done, so we can *always* come to Him and find mercy.

> We can always draw near to Jesus, drink deeply of His meekness, and let Him teach us how to let it flow more fully through us.

Donald Gee referred to this as "going with Christ through the school of meekness [gentleness]."[37] I like that phrase! It reminds us that, just as in the natural, if we want to do well in school, we have to study and be diligent. If we want to excel in meekness, we must do the same. Even though we have the Source of meekness living inside us, it's not just going to automatically take over our lives.

No, to develop in meekness we must renew our minds in that area. We must continue to focus on it and study it in the Word.

Although that will take effort, I encourage you to go for it. More importantly, so does the Word of God. It commands us time and again:

> Walk worthy of the vocation wherewith ye are called, with all lowliness and meekness (Ephesians 4:1-2).

---

37 Gee, *The Fruit of the Spirit,* 58.

Put on therefore, as the elect of God, holy and beloved, bowels of mercies, kindness, humbleness of mind, meekness (Colossians 3:12).

Let nothing be done through strife or vainglory; but in lowliness of mind [or meekness] let each esteem other[s] better than themselves (Philippians 2:3).

Follow after righteousness, godliness, faith, love, patience, meekness (1 Timothy 6:11).

If a man be overtaken in a fault, ye which are spiritual, restore such an one in the spirit of meekness (Galatians 6:1).

Speak evil of no man, to be no brawlers, but gentle, showing all meekness unto all men (Titus 3:2).

Receive with meekness the engrafted word, which is able to save your souls (James 1:21).

Sanctify the Lord God in your hearts: and be ready always to give an answer to every man that asketh you a reason of the hope that is in you with meekness (1 Peter 3:15).

Let it be the hidden man of the heart, in that which is not corruptible, even the ornament of a meek and quiet spirit, which is in the sight of God of great price (1 Peter 3:4).

Speak Your Faith

I choose to put on and walk in the fruit of meekness. I am not self-assertive. I am not self-centered. I receive with meekness the engrafted Word. Like Jesus, I treat others in humility and love. I humble myself before God. I let go of my own way, and I take up His way. I submit to God, and I am happy and quick to do what He says. I have a teachable and submissive spirit, therefore, I walk in God's wisdom!

Chapter 14

GOING FOR ETERNAL GOLD

All athletes practice strict self-control. They do it to win a prize that will fade away, but we do it for an eternal prize.

1 CORINTHIANS 9:25, NLT-96

I'm not sure if there's a reason the Apostle Paul put temperance last when he listed the nine fruit of the spirit, but for the purposes of this study, I'm glad he did! I can't think of anything I'd rather talk about in the final chapter of this book.

Temperance, or as it's also translated, *self-control,* serves as an appropriate finale because it affects all the other forces of the spirit. It helps us control our natural, physical tendencies so that love, joy, peace, patience, kindness, goodness, faithfulness and meekness can flow in our lives unhindered. It helps us maintain our walk in the spirit by enabling us to keep our bodies in check.

Keeping your body in check is vital because left to itself, your flesh doesn't have good sense! Unlike your spirit, it didn't change when you were born again. It stayed the same, so if it's not brought under your spirit's control, it will just keep on doing what it did before you were saved. It will conform to whatever it's exposed to, give in to the suggestions of the devil, and yield to the pressures of this fallen world. It will pull you right back into sin.

We've already seen in Galatians 5 what the works of the flesh are. They include things like "immorality, impurity, indecency, idolatry, sorcery, enmity, strife, jealousy, anger (ill temper), selfishness, divisions...envy, drunkenness, carousing, and the like" (Galatians 5:19-21, AMPC).

Those things are deadly! They wreak havoc in people's lives. But the spiritual force of self-control can handle every one of them. It can dominate even the strongest physical cravings and desires and make your body behave when it's tempted to get out of line.

When your body wants to sleep another hour in the morning instead of getting up early to pray, self-control can get it out of bed. When your body wants you to listen to, look at, say or do something you know you shouldn't, self-control can restrain it. When the devil tempts you to give in to destructive natural impulses—to eat like a glutton, pass along a piece of gossip, get involved with pornography, alcohol, drugs or immorality—self-control can shut down that temptation by saying *no!*

Even in the midst of a world that says doing whatever your flesh wants is all right, the fruit of self-control can empower you to live a holy lifestyle. It can bring your outward man into line with your inward man, so instead of doing the works of the flesh, you're able to use your body "as an instrument to do what is right for the glory of God" (Romans 6:13, NLT).

Self-control is defined by Webster's dictionary as "possessing power, strong, having mastery or possession of, continent, or having restraint of one's self or one's actions or feelings."

Self-control is inward strength that's greater than all the outward strength of temptation, desire or excitement.

When used in a strictly natural context, self-control refers to a strength that's generated completely by human willpower. But in spiritual context, it refers to something much more. It is the outworking of God's life in the believer, and a will backed by the same strength and power that raised Jesus from the dead and exalted Him in heaven!

That supernatural strength and power resides in the spirit of every born-again Christian, so it's equally available to us all. It can be cultivated not only by believers whose wills are naturally forceful, but also by those who tend to be weak-willed and lacking in discipline. That's a game changer, particularly for believers who, in the past, have repeatedly lost battles with their flesh! As Donald Gee wrote:

> To teach self-control to a man or a woman who has by years of self-indulgence lost all the power of either physical, mental, or spiritual resistance seems little short of cruel mockery. To such a person, the message of the fruit of the Spirit is good news indeed. It means that Christ within us can accomplish what we can never hope to do in our own strength. It also means that continuously walking with Him will change the weakest of us into His image until people will begin to see in us something of that superb self-control, and divine balance in every situation that always marked the Son of Man. The inward strength is not ours— it is His.[38]

First John 4:4 says that greater is He who is in us, than he who is in the world!

---

38 Gee, *The Fruit of the Spirit*, 64.

WALKING IN THE FRUIT OF THE SPIRIT

Imagine, for a moment, walking in the kind of self-control Jesus displayed when He was on earth. Imagine always being the master of your body and never letting it have the mastery over you. That would be marvelous, wouldn't it? And though it might sound impossible to our natural minds, that's exactly what God has called us to do. He said it clearly in the Bible:

> Be self-controlled (1 Thessalonians 5:8, NIV-84).
>
> Say "No" to ungodliness and worldly passions, and…live self-controlled, upright and godly lives in this present age (Titus 2:12, NIV-84).
>
> Walk in the same manner as [Jesus] walked (1 John 2:6, NASB).

Those aren't just nice suggestions. They're scriptural commands, and as lofty as they may seem, we've been spiritually equipped to obey them. As Greg Zoschak said in his book *A Call for Character:*

> God would not demand of His children that which would be impossible for them to fulfill. He never intended for believers to overcome the flesh by their flesh. Rather, God has provided His children with a supernatural seed of strength and self-control. That seed only requires cultivation in order for it to produce overcoming power by the Spirit. This power will surpass all previous, unsuccessful attempts at self-improvement.[39]

Think of it! We don't have to try to control our flesh by natural human effort. We have Christ within us accomplishing what we could never do in our own strength. We have the power of self-control flowing out of our spirits that isn't just ours, it's His.

---

39   Zoschak, *A Call for Character,* 218.

> As believers, we don't have to keep trying and failing in our own strength to get our fleshly habits and appetites under control.

His power in us never fails! It will enable us to overcome ungodly habits and fleshly tendencies that, on our own, we've been powerless to resist. It will give us the strength to successfully discipline our flesh even in areas where, in the natural, we're very weak.

What's more, as we continue to yield to it, over time, the supernatural force of self-control will actually affect us in the natural. It will train us physically so that our bodies get out of the habit of doing bad things and into the habit of going for the things of God. Then, instead of remaining fleshy spiritual babies, we'll mature in the Lord. We'll become "full-grown" believers "whose senses and mental faculties are trained by practice to discriminate and distinguish between what is morally good and noble and what is evil" (Hebrews 5:14, AMPC).

Living in Dangerous Days

If you want to see how important such training is, think about the believers you've known who've fallen prey to the lusts of their flesh and ruined their lives. Think about the sad stories you've heard about Christians who got caught up in things like pornography or adultery, spent themselves into bankruptcy, or got addicted to drugs or alcohol. Every one of those sad stories can be traced back to a lack of self-control. They all began when someone gave in to the flesh and decided, *I'm going to indulge in this,* even though that person knew it wasn't right.

Rarely has anyone ever been sucked into some kind of fleshly addiction thinking, *This is a good thing to do.* Most people knew better from the start, but they indulged anyway. They thought, *I'll just do it this one time.* Then one time led to another and, eventually, it got control of their lives. They wound up sowing to the flesh, and just like Galatians 6:8 says, from the flesh they reaped destruction.

The force of self-control can prevent such tragedies! It strengthens us in those moments of decision so that our stories end up being glad ones instead of sad ones. It helps us make the right choices and empowers us to keep sowing to the spirit so we can keep reaping abundant life.

That's not easy to do—particularly in this day and age. We're living in what the Bible calls *the last days*. The devil's time is about to run out, and he's working harder than ever before to push this world further into darkness. He's constantly promoting sin and the lusts of the flesh on every media platform—television, movies, radio, internet, music, newspapers, magazines and every form of social media. He's using every means he can to convince Christians, and non-Christians alike, to surrender to the lusts of the flesh so he can move into their lives and take control.

We're seeing, in our day, the fulfillment of what Paul prophesied in 2 Timothy 3: "In the last days perilous times will come: For men will be lovers of themselves, lovers of money, boasters, proud, blasphemers, disobedient to parents, unthankful, unholy, unloving, unforgiving, slanderers, without self-control, brutal, despisers of good, traitors, headstrong, haughty, lovers of pleasure rather than lovers of God, having a form of godliness but denying its power" (verses 1-5, NKJV).

We hear news reports every day about people who fit that description. We even see some of them featured on TV talk shows. Sometimes, when I'm switching through the television channels, I wonder where on earth they find those people. I think, *Why would they be willing to tell the whole world about all the rotten things their family members do to one another?*

This world is teeming with people whose lives are out of control. People will do anything that feels good to their flesh, as long as they can get away with it. Most of them wouldn't be willing to go on TV and confess to it, but they're all around us. Second Timothy 3:5 (NKJV) says, "From such people turn away!"

That's good advice. If you want to grow in the spirit and develop the fruit of self-control, don't hang around with people who are ruled by their flesh. Love them, be kind to them, and share Jesus with them when the opportunity arises. But don't spend a great deal of time with them because the more you associate with people who lack self-control, the easier it will become for you to indulge in things that aren't right. So, choose your associations wisely. Let their temperance and self-control inspire you to walk in more of that fruit yourself.

Find friends who are more spiritual than you are, and whose lives are full of the fruit of the spirit.

Jesus is coming back soon! When He arrives, you don't want Him to find you living like the world and being ruled by your flesh. You want to be walking in the spirit, so Jesus finds you spiritually alert and ready to go.

For that to happen, though, you have to live as if the last trumpet might sound at any moment, looking forward to the day when Jesus returns, and following the instructions He gave us in Luke 21:

> Take heed to yourselves and be on your guard, lest your hearts be overburdened and depressed (weighed down) with the giddiness and headache and nausea of self-indulgence, drunkenness, and worldly worries and cares pertaining to [the business of] this life, and [lest] that day come upon you suddenly like a trap or a noose; for it will come upon all who live upon the face of the entire earth. Keep awake then and watch at all times [be discreet, attentive, and ready], praying that you may have the full strength and ability and be accounted worthy

to escape all these things...and to stand in the presence of the Son of Man (verses 34-36, AMPC).

Jesus didn't mince words in those verses. He warned us very plainly that in these last days, controlling our flesh would be crucial. It will help us stay out of the devil's snares. It will enable us to live in a way that's worthy of the Lord, so when He comes back for us we can stand in His presence unashamed!

"Well," someone might say, "I don't like to think about Jesus coming back. It scares me."

Then you haven't been living like you know you should. You've been overindulging your flesh and doing some things you shouldn't be doing. Turn that around, and your attitude will change. When your spirit is in dominion, and you're living a temperate, godly lifestyle, you'll get excited about the fact that Jesus is coming soon. You'll think it's the best news you've ever heard!

That's certainly what the Apostle Paul thought. He called the coming of the Lord a source of hope and comfort. He said it's like a guiding light that keeps us spiritually awake and on the right path. It helps us live in holiness and not in the passion of lust, like the heathen who don't know God.

Paul also told us we should understand and be aware of exactly what's going to happen when Jesus returns:

> I do not want you to be ignorant, brethren, concerning those who have fallen asleep, lest you sorrow as others who have no hope.... For this we say to you by the word of the Lord, that we who are alive and remain until the coming of the Lord will by no means precede those who are asleep. For the Lord Himself will descend from heaven with a shout, with the voice of an archangel, and with the trumpet of God. And the dead in

Christ will rise first. Then we who are alive and remain shall be caught up together with them in the clouds to meet the Lord in the air. And thus we shall always be with the Lord. Therefore comfort one another with these words.... But you, brethren, are not in darkness, so that this Day should overtake you as a thief. You are all sons of light and sons of the day. We are not of the night nor of darkness. Therefore let us not sleep, as others do, but let us watch and be sober. For those who sleep, sleep at night, and those who get drunk are drunk at night. But let us who are of the day be sober, putting on the breastplate of faith and love, and as a helmet the hope of salvation. For God did not appoint us to wrath, but to obtain salvation through our Lord Jesus Christ, who died for us, that whether we wake or sleep, we should live together with Him. Therefore comfort each other and edify one another, just as you also are doing (1 Thessalonians 4:13, 15-18; 5:4-11, NKJV).

Look again at what Paul told us to do so we would be ready for the coming of the Lord. He said, "let us *watch.*" That's the same word Jesus used in Luke 21:36 and Mark 13:33, when He was teaching about the day of His return:

Take heed, watch and pray; for you do not know when the time [for My return] is. It is like a man going to a far country, who left his house and gave authority to his servants, and to each his work, and commanded the doorkeeper to watch. Watch therefore, for you do not know when the master of the house is coming—in the evening, at midnight, at the crowing of the rooster, or in the morning—lest, coming suddenly, he find you sleeping. And what I say to you, I say to all: Watch! (Mark 13:33-37, NKJV).

The Greek word translated *watch* means "to be sleepless, i.e. Keep awake."[40] So, when Jesus and Paul said *watch,* they were saying, "Guard yourselves and be on the lookout to do what's right. Stay awake to the effects this ungodly world can have on your body. Don't live a lazy life and just do the things that are convenient. Discipline your flesh, and go after the things of God!"

Overindulging Can Cost You

As I've emphasized throughout this book, the primary way you go after God is by attending to His Word. His Word keeps you mindful of Him and His ways.

> *God's Word strengthens your spirit, so you will obey Him and stay on the right track.*

If you get too busy for the Word, and let other things fill your heart, your spirit will inevitably take a back seat and your flesh will take over. You'll become like the thorny-ground people in Jesus' parable of the sower. They heard the Word, but "then the cares and anxieties of the world and distractions of the age, and the pleasure and delight and false glamour and deceitfulness of riches, and the craving and passionate desire for other things creep in and choke and suffocate the Word, and it becomes fruitless" (Mark 4:19, AMPC).

It's easy to let that happen, especially with all the technology we have available to us in our generation. We have more things to distract us today than people ever had before. We have the internet, TV, computers, smartphones and other devices that broadcast news and entertainment all day and all night. We have video games, social media, cars, trucks, four-wheelers, motorcycles, airplanes and boats, hobbies galore, and all kinds of different sports. All these things can keep us very busy.

40 *Strong's Exhaustive Concordance of the Bible,* G69.

With all these things easily available, it's hard not to overindulge in them. It's tempting to think that because, in themselves, they aren't sinful, we can spend as much time on them as we want, and it won't affect our walk with God.

The Bible tells us, however, that's not exactly accurate. It says, "Everything is permissible for me, but not all things are beneficial. Everything is permissible for me, but I will not be enslaved by anything [and brought under its power, allowing it to control me]" (1 Corinthians 6:12, AMP).

Obviously, it's not lawful, or right, for us to do things that are specifically taught against in the Scriptures. But, according to that verse, even things that *are* lawful for us can become a problem if we overindulge in them. If they start ruling over our bodies, or we begin giving them some of the time and attention we should be giving to God, they'll get us over into the flesh realm and sap our spiritual power.

Take hobbies, for instance. It's OK to have them, but we don't want to get so caught up in them that we live for them. We don't want our hobbies to become so important to us that we think about them more than we do the Lord. We want to yield to the force of temperance and keep those things in their right place.

When we do that, we can enjoy hobbies and other fun things in moderation while making sure we don't give them too much attention. We can maintain our priorities, keep God and His Word first place in our lives, and be like the good-ground people in the parable of the sower "who hear the word, accept it, and bear fruit: some thirtyfold, some sixty, and some a hundred" (Mark 4:20, NKJV).

The more the Word of God bears fruit in our lives, the more we'll grow spiritually and the more self-controlled we'll become. The more self-controlled we become, the easier it is to keep our priorities straight. It's a cycle, and it all revolves around hearing God's Word and obeying it.

That's why Jesus said at the end of His parable, "Be careful what you are hearing. The measure [of thought and study] you give [to the truth you hear] will be the measure [of virtue and knowledge] that comes back to you—and more [besides] will be given to you *who hear*. For to him who has will more be given; and from him who has nothing, even what he has will be taken away" (verse 24-25, AMPC).

What you're hearing is key! If you're not happy with your spiritual life, change what you're seeing and hearing. If you're being overcome by natural distractions, and fleshly interests are taking over your affections, take more time to hear and attend to the Word.

Your desire follows your attention!

Speak Your Faith

My desire follows my attention. I desire God's Word. I meditate on it day and night, so I make my way prosperous and have good success. I keep God's Word in front of my eyes and in my ears. I hear God's Word and do it. According to Philippians 2:13, I declare that God is at work in me both to will and to do of His good pleasure. I desire God's Word, and it is working in me mightily!

People who come to our Believers' Conventions testify to the truth of their desire following their attention. They tell us that after they sit there listening to the Word day and night for almost a week, things that seemed important to them before the meetings started don't seem like a big deal anymore. They're not thinking about the problems at the office. They're not thinking about the movies they want to see or the new golf clubs they've been admiring. Their hearts become set on the things of

God because they've been hearing His Word, and their attention has been on Him.

This is the secret to becoming a person of strong self-control! You make hearing the Word of God a habit in your life—and when you hear it, you latch onto it. You receive it, and act on it. You reverence and respond to it. You begin to realize, *This is God talking to me!*

I know people who, before they were born again, had almost no self-control. They overindulged in everything. They overate, smoked and drank. They did whatever their flesh wanted to do the moment it wanted to do it. They didn't even change their lifestyle very much after they were born again and filled with the Holy Spirit. But when they began studying the Word and growing in God, before long, they were changed. They had developed real self-control.

That's how we develop all the fruit of the spirit. It's just how the process works! We become partakers of the divine nature through the new birth, then grow up spiritually by feeding on and obeying God's Word. We put the things of God first place in our lives, apply ourselves to them and, as we do, our born-again inward nature begins to manifest outwardly in our lives.

For this very reason, make every effort to add to your faith goodness; and to goodness, knowledge; and to knowledge, self-control; and to self-control, perseverance; and to perseverance, godliness; and to godliness, brotherly kindness; and to brotherly kindness, love. For if you possess these qualities in increasing measure, they will keep you from being ineffective and unproductive in your knowledge of our Lord Jesus Christ. But if anyone does not have them, he is nearsighted and blind, and has forgotten that he has been cleansed from his past sins. Therefore, my brothers, be all the more eager to make your calling and election sure. For if you do these things, you will never fall (2 Peter 1:5-10, NIV-84).

I don't want to fall, do you? Even though I know if I did fall, God would forgive me, most likely my fall would affect others and possibly cause them to stumble. People aren't usually as quick to forgive our fleshly failures as God is. They tend to remember the bad things we did and hold them against us. Sometimes, they even make it their personal mission to never let *us* forget them.

But more than all those things, my heart's desire is to please God. I desire to do what He wants me to do—to fulfill His plan for my life and to finish the race He's called me to run, with joy!

Increasing Your Spiritual Strength and Sensitivity

"Gloria, are you saying we have to be perfectly self-controlled if we're going to finish our race in God?"

No, I don't know of any believer who's arrived at a place of perfect self-control. We all miss it at times and have to repent. But the more we grow up spiritually, the less often we'll have to do so. Not only do we become spiritually stronger, but our conscience develops and becomes more sensitive to what grieves the Spirit of God.

Where we once might have spoken bad things about someone, without even noticing or thinking it was sin, we begin realizing such talk displeases the Lord. Where once we may have watched vulgar, profanity-filled movies or TV shows without being bothered by them, we'll turn them off because they violate our hearts. We're not "nearsighted and blind" anymore, as we were when we were spiritual babies (2 Peter 1:9, NIV). We will have become more discerning and, as a result, operate at a higher level of self-control and victory.

"But I've always been impulsive!" someone might say, "I've tried to be more self-controlled, but I'm just naturally the kind of person who reacts to whatever is going on at the moment."

Then stop seeing yourself in the natural, and look at yourself after the spirit. See yourself as God sees you. Say what He says about you. Instead of thinking and talking about yourself as if you're unable to control your actions and emotions, focus on the Spirit of God inside you, and declare His Word over yourself.

God said He hasn't given you "a spirit of timidity, but a spirit of power, of love and of self-discipline" (2 Timothy 1:7, NIV-84). He said the One who is in you "is greater than he who is in the world" (1 John 4:4, NKJV). He said, "If any man be in Christ, he is a new creature: old things are passed away; behold, all things are become new. And all things are of God" (2 Corinthians 5:17-18).

The new birth is the great equalizer.

It re-creates you in God's image and puts in you everything that's in Him. You just have to spend time in the Word, find out what's in you, and dare to believe it.

If you have an addiction of some kind—like overeating, smoking or gossiping—find scriptures that speak to you about the victory and dominion God has given you. Meditate on verses like Ephesians 6:10 that says, "Be strong in the Lord, and in the power of his might." Rehearse them over and over, and practice saying them to yourself.

Speak Your Faith

I'm strong because God is strong, and He's inside me. I am born of Him. The same power that's in Him is in me. There is nothing that can overcome His power inside me. So I boldly declare that I am an overcomer. I am strong in the Lord, and in the power of His might (Ephesians 6:10)!

I used to say those things a lot when I was first born again because I'd always been timid and quiet. I didn't have a very strong self-image, so I was greatly encouraged to find out I didn't have to depend on myself anymore. I was thrilled to learn from the Word of God that all I had to do was believe and obey God and let His power in my born-again spirit flow out!

To be clear, when you feed on the things of God, strength and spiritual force will come into your soul and your will, and you'll be able to hold fast and not waver. The human will, which is part of the soul, is a crucial part of the process. Your will is your "chooser," your "decider." It makes the call when you have to choose between doing something God's way or the world's way, between indulging your flesh or crucifying it.

When your will is enlightened by God's Word and backed by the power of your born-again spirit, it helps you to make the right call and then follow through. It helps you choose to continually walk in the spirit and not in the flesh.

For example, out of the blue, someone may do something ugly to you that makes you angry. Your will immediately engages and determines, almost instantly, how you're going to respond. If you have the Word strongly planted in your heart, and you've been spending time with the Lord, it will yield to your spirit. It will put the brakes on your flesh and say, "Be angry and sin not!"

On the other hand, if you've been living a carnal life, your will won't have the power of your spirit behind it. Before you even have time to think, it will make the wrong choice and you'll fly off the handle, saying or doing something you'll regret.

Proverbs 14:17 says, "A quick-tempered man does foolish things…", (NIV-84). So, when your will is backed by the fruit of self-control, it will keep you from getting into trouble. It will empower you to "walk circumspectly [in victory], not as fools, but as wise" (Ephesians 5:15).

Train Like an Olympian

The fruit of self-control can make a tremendous difference in how you finish your spiritual race! Without it, you'll wander off course and squander your time and energy on fleshly indulgences. You won't accomplish everything you're called by God to do, and you'll miss out on some of your eternal rewards and blessings in this life also.

Those rewards are precious! They're well worth disciplining your flesh to enable you to receive them because they're not just temporal—they last forever.

Think about all the work and dedication people often put into winning a sports event or some kind of medal. Olympic athletes, for example, discipline their bodies for years, sacrificing all kinds of fleshly indulgences. They stick to special diets and tell their flesh, "You can't eat that junk food. It's not good for you." They train when it's comfortable and when it's uncomfortable, when it's convenient and when it's not. They so dedicate themselves to their sport that their lives revolve around it.

I heard one Olympian, a Spirit-filled believer who won a gold medal in track, say that to get in shape she ran every day for years, no matter how adverse the conditions. She ran in the rain and in the cold. She would push herself so hard sometimes that her body would give out and she couldn't go another step. Why? Because she was determined to do whatever it took to win the prize!

When I heard her interview, I was reminded of the attitude of the Apostle Paul when it came to fulfilling his spiritual calling. I thought about how he disciplined his body and sacrificed fleshly indulgences. He said in 1 Corinthians 9:

> Do you not know that in a race all the runners compete, but [only] one receives the prize? So run [your race] that you may lay hold [of the prize] and make it yours. Now every athlete who goes into training conducts himself temperately and restricts himself in all things. They do it to win a wreath that will soon wither, but we [do it to receive a crown of eternal blessedness] that cannot wither. Therefore I do not run uncertainly (without definite aim). I do not box like one beating the air and striking without an adversary. But [like a boxer] I buffet my body [handle it roughly, discipline it by hardships] and subdue it, for fear that after proclaiming to others the Gospel and things pertaining to it, I myself should become unfit [not stand the test, be unapproved and rejected as a counterfeit] (verses 24-27, AMPC).

Paul had some amazing spiritual experiences. He saw Jesus on the road to Damascus. He saw visions and received great revelations from God. But, just like us, he lived in a natural body. To complete the mission God had given him, he had to keep that body under control—and he had to do it while going through some extremely difficult circumstances.

Paul spent a great deal of time in prison for preaching the gospel. (You think prison is bad now, think how much worse it must have been back then!) He was beaten, severely whipped three different times, shackled, stoned and left for dead, shipwrecked and stranded at sea. Yet he learned to walk in the spirit in the midst of it all. He learned to keep his flesh in check so that in every situation (even when he was sitting in a Philippian jail, bruised and bleeding) he could keep right on praising God.

As a result, Paul finished his race as a winner! At the end of his life, he was able to write:

> I am now ready to be offered, and the time of my departure is at hand. I have fought a good fight, I have finished my course, I have kept the faith: Henceforth there is laid up for me a crown of righteousness, which the Lord, the righteous judge, shall give me at that day: and not to me only, but unto all them also that love his appearing (2 Timothy 4:6-8).

That's what we all want to be able to say as believers when our race on earth is over! We want to be able to say, "I'm out of here. I'm going to get my crown!" But to do so, we'll have to follow Paul's example. We'll have to discipline our flesh.

Of course, we'll probably have an easier go of it than he did. He had a special calling. He was responsible for preaching the gospel to the gentiles in the entire known world, which meant he had to make extraordinary sacrifices.

Most of us won't ever face those kind of things. We aren't likely to be required to physically die for Jesus. But if we're truly going to live for Him, there will be some dying involved—dying to our own welfare, ambitions and fleshly desires. In other words, we will have to obey the instructions Jesus gave in Mark 8:34 where He said, "If anyone would come after me, he must deny himself and take up his cross and follow me" (NIV-84).

What exactly does it mean to take up your cross?

It definitely doesn't mean, as religious tradition teaches, that you have to give up all the good things in life. It doesn't mean you have to go around with a long face and put up with poverty, sickness and disease, as if they were your cross to bear. That would be unscriptural. The Bible says God gives us richly all things to enjoy (1 Timothy 6:17). It says God wants us to prosper and be in health even as our souls prosper (3 John 2). So, Jesus doesn't want you to deny yourself those things that He already paid the price for you to receive.

> *Taking up your cross is yielding to the fruit of self-control and crucifying every fleshly desire that is contrary to God's will and His Word.*

You have to say, "No, flesh! You're not going to get your way!" and take dominion over your body or your emotions when they want to do something other than what the Spirit of God tells you to do.

Say, for example, you have a successful business and God calls you into full-time ministry. Answering that call would probably be a little hard on your flesh. You might have to take up your cross by shutting the door on that business and enrolling in Bible school. You might have to deny yourself by taking a temporary pay cut, trusting God with your finances, and being patient with unsaved relatives who think you've lost your mind.

Those kinds of things can be tough in the natural! But the powerful force of self-control that flows out of your spirit will empower you to do them. It will help you maintain your joy and stay focused on the eternal prize set before you. It will enable you to go on with God, even when your flesh has to suffer, so that you can finish your course the way the New Testament tells us that Moses did:

> He preferred to share the oppression [suffer the hardships] and bear the shame of the people of God rather than to have the fleeting enjoyment of a sinful life. He considered the contempt and abuse and shame [borne for] the Christ (the Messiah Who was to come) to be greater wealth than all the treasures of Egypt, for he looked forward and away to the

reward (recompense).... he never flinched but held staunchly to his purpose and endured steadfastly as one who gazed on Him Who is invisible (Hebrews 11:25-27, AMPC).

Therefore then, since we are surrounded by so great a cloud of witnesses [who have borne testimony to the Truth], let us strip off and throw aside every encumbrance (unnecessary weight) and that sin which so readily (deftly and cleverly) clings to and entangles us, and let us run with patient endurance and steady and active persistence the appointed course of the race that is set before us, looking away [from all that will distract] to Jesus, Who is the Leader and the Source of our faith [giving the first incentive for our belief] and is also its Finisher [bringing it to maturity and perfection]. He, for the joy [of obtaining the prize] that was set before Him, endured the cross, despising and ignoring the shame, and is now seated at the right hand of the throne of God (Hebrews 12:1-2, AMPC).

This is how all God's faith champions live! It's how all of us, as believers, are called to run our race! We do it by walking in the spirit and crucifying the flesh. We look away from everything that would distract us, keeping our eyes on Jesus, and joyfully anticipating our eternal reward.

We don't live like the world does, just for the pleasure of this present moment. And we don't go after just what feels good to our flesh right now. People who don't know God have to do that because, to them, this natural existence is all that's important. They have to get all the gratification they can right now because this brief time here on earth is the best they'll ever see.

On the other hand, believers are just getting started on eternity! The years we spend here on earth (even though they're filled with God's blessings) will be the worst we'll ever see.

> *We're just sojourners on assignment as God's
> ambassadors to do a job.*

After we leave here, we'll get to live in a wonderful place called heaven and spend eternity in the presence of God.

Let's say, as Paul did:

> But what things were gain to me, these I have counted loss for Christ. Yet indeed I also count all things loss for the excellence of the knowledge of Christ Jesus my Lord, for whom I have suffered the loss of all things, and count them as rubbish, that I may gain Christ and be found in Him, not having my own righteousness, which is from the law, but that which is through faith in Christ, the righteousness which is from God by faith; that I may know Him and the power of His resurrection, and the fellowship of His sufferings, being conformed to His death, if, by any means, I may attain to the resurrection from the dead. Not that I have already attained, or am already perfected; but I press on, that I may lay hold of that for which Christ Jesus has also laid hold of me. Brethren, I do not count myself to have apprehended; but one thing I do, forgetting those things which are behind and reaching forward to those things which are ahead, I press toward the goal for the prize of the upward call of God in Christ Jesus (Philippians 3:7-14, NKJV).

While we're on this earth, let's concentrate on getting our job done. Let's yield to the force of self-control and all the other fruit of the spirit. Let's stop looking back at the old things of the flesh, and let's "press toward the goal for the prize of the upward call of God in Christ Jesus"!

Prayer for Salvation and Baptism in the Holy Spirit

Heavenly Father, I come to You in the Name of Jesus. Your Word says, "Whosoever shall call on the name of the Lord shall be saved" (Acts 2:21). I am calling on You. I pray and ask Jesus to come into my heart and be Lord over my life according to Romans 10:9-10: "If thou shalt confess with thy mouth the Lord Jesus, and shalt believe in thine heart that God hath raised him from the dead, thou shalt be saved. For with the heart man believeth unto righteousness; and with the mouth confession is made unto salvation." I do that now. I confess that Jesus is Lord, and I believe in my heart that God raised Him from the dead. I repent of sin. I renounce it. I renounce the devil and everything he stands for. Jesus is my Lord.

I am now reborn! I am a Christian—a child of Almighty God! I am saved! You also said in Your Word, "If ye then, being evil, know how to give good gifts unto your children: HOW MUCH MORE shall your heavenly Father give the Holy Spirit to them that ask him?" (Luke 11:13). I'm also asking You to fill me with the Holy Spirit. Holy Spirit, rise up within me as I praise God. I fully expect to speak with other tongues as You give me the utterance (Acts 2:4). In Jesus' Name. Amen!

Begin to praise God for filling you with the Holy Spirit and power. Speak those words and syllables you receive—not in your own language, but the language given to you by the Holy Spirit. You have to use your own voice. God will not force you to speak. Don't be concerned with how it sounds. It is a heavenly language!

Continue with the blessing God has given you and pray in the spirit, by the Spirit, every day.

You are a born-again, Spirit-filled believer. You'll never be the same!

Find a good church that boldly preaches God's Word and obeys it. Become part of a church family who will love and care for you as you love and care for them.

We need to be connected to each other. It increases our strength in God. It's God's plan for us.

Make it a habit to read the Bible every day and watch VICTORY Channel™. Become a doer of the Word, who is blessed in his doing (James 1:22-25).

Jesus Is Lord!

Gloria Copeland

ABOUT THE AUTHOR

Gloria Copeland is a noted author and minister of the gospel whose teaching ministry is known throughout the world. Believers worldwide know her through Believers' Conventions, Victory Campaigns, magazine articles, teaching audios and videos, and the daily and Sunday *Believer's Voice of Victory* television broadcast, which she hosts with her husband, Kenneth Copeland. She is known for Healing School, which she began teaching and hosting in 1979 at KCM meetings. Gloria delivers the Word of God and the keys to victorious Christian living to millions of people every year.

Gloria is author of the New York Times best-seller, *God's Master Plan for Your Life* and *Live Long, Finish Strong,* as well as numerous other favorites, including *God's Will for You, Walk With God, God's Will Is Prosperity, Hidden Treasures* and *To Know Him.* She has also co-authored several books with her husband, including *Family Promises, Healing Promises* and the best-selling daily devotionals, *From Faith to Faith* and *Pursuit of His Presence.*

She holds an honorary doctorate from Oral Roberts University. In 1994, Gloria was voted Christian Woman of the Year, an honor conferred on women whose example demonstrates outstanding Christian leadership. Gloria is also the co-founder and vice president of Kenneth Copeland Ministries in Fort Worth, Texas.

BELIEVER'S VOICE OF VICTORY

When the Lord first spoke to Kenneth and Gloria Copeland about starting the *Believer's Voice of Victory* magazine...

He said: *This is your seed. Give it to everyone who ever responds to your ministry, and don't ever allow anyone to pay for a subscription!*

For more than 50 years, it has been the joy of Kenneth Copeland Ministries to bring the good news to believers. Readers enjoy teaching from ministers who write from lives of living contact with God, and testimonies from believers experiencing victory through God's Word in their everyday lives.

Today, the *BVOV* magazine is mailed monthly, bringing encouragement and blessing to believers around the world. Many even use it as a ministry tool, passing it on to others who desire to know Jesus and grow in their faith!

Request your **FREE** subscription to the
Believer's Voice of Victory magazine today!

Go to **freevictory.com** to subscribe online, or call us at
1-800-600-7395 (U.S. only) or **+1-817-852-6000**.

WE'RE HERE FOR YOU!®

Your growth in God's Word and your victory in Jesus are at the very center of our hearts. In every way God has equipped us, we will help you deal with the issues facing you, so you can be the **victorious overcomer** He has planned for you to be.

The mission of Kenneth Copeland Ministries is about all of us growing and going together. Our prayer is that you will take full advantage of all the Lord has given us to share with you.

Wherever you are in the world, you can watch the *Believer's Voice of Victory* broadcast on our VICTORY Channel™ on DISH® and DIRECTV® (check your local listings), Roku®, YouTube®, Apple TV®, and Amazon Fire TV or on the GoVictory mobile app. Our website, **kcm.org,** gives you access to every resource we've developed for your victory. And, you can find contact information for our international offices in Africa, Australia, Canada, Europe, Ukraine, South America and our headquarters in the United States.

Each office is staffed with devoted men and women, ready to serve and pray with you. You can contact the worldwide office nearest you for assistance, and you can call us for prayer at our U.S. number, +1-817-852-6000, every day of the week!

We encourage you to connect with us often and let us be part of your everyday walk of faith!

JESUS IS LORD!